The Power of a
PRAYING®
Mom

STORMIE
OMARTIAN

HARVEST HOUSE PUBLISHERS
EUGENE, OREGON

All Scripture quotations are from the New King James Version®. Copyright © 1982 by Thomas Nelson, Inc. Used by permission. All rights reserved.

Cover by Harvest House Publishers, Eugene, Oregon

Cover illustration © Komar art / Shutterstock

Back cover author photo © by Michael Gomez Photography

THE POWER OF A PRAYING is a registered trademark of The Hawkins Children's LLC. Harvest House Publishers, Inc., is the exclusive licensee of the federally registered trademark THE POWER OF A PRAYING.

Some of the material in this book has been taken from
    The Power of a Praying® *Parent Book of Prayers*
    The Power of a Praying® *Woman Book of Prayers*
    The Power of Praying® *for Your Adult Children Book of Prayers*
    30 Days to Becoming a Woman of Prayer Book of Prayers

THE POWER OF A PRAYING® MOM

Copyright © 2015 by Stormie Omartian
Published by Harvest House Publishers
Eugene, Oregon 97402
www.harvesthousepublishers.com

ISBN 978-0-7369-6599-6 (pbk.)
ISBN 978-0-7369-6600-9 (eBook)

Printed in China

    15 16 17 18 19 20 21 22 23 / RDS-JH / 10 9 8 7 6 5 4 3 2 1

Contents

Introduction

I have noticed that many moms pray often for their children, but they don't always pray for themselves. And they need to. That's because an important part of being a good mom is recognizing that you can't do it well without God's help. We moms need the Lord to enable us every day to produce the fruit of the Spirit, which is "love, joy, peace, longsuffering, kindness, goodness, faithfulness, gentleness, self-control" (Galatians 5:22-23). Who doesn't need every bit of that when raising children?

Who doesn't need a closer walk with God so that you can partner with Him in prayer to positively affect each child's life and be guided by Him in every decision and thought? It's important that we moms pray for ourselves to become our best in order to help our children become their best.

Most of the prayers here are excerpted from my four books of prayer listed on the copyright page of this book. I have also written some original material as well. The prayers are laid out in a way that helps you pray for yourself and your child at the same time. So the prayer you see on the left page will be a prayer for *you*, with space to write down any specifics you want to remember to pray for yourself. The page opposite of that on the right is a prayer for *your child*, also with space to write any specifics.

I pray you will find this way of praying as valuable to you as I have, and you will see, sense, and feel the increasing benefits to both you and your children.

Stormie Omartian

Until now you have asked nothing in My name.
Ask, and you will receive, that your joy may be full.

JOHN 16:24

❧

For this child I prayed,
and the Lord has granted me
my petition which I asked of Him.

1 SAMUEL 1:27

Lord, Draw Me into a Closer Walk with You

Draw near to God and He will draw near to you.

JAMES 4:8

Lord, help me to set aside time each day to meet with You alone. As I come before You, teach me to pray the way You want me to. Help me to learn more about You. Lord, You have said, "If anyone thirsts, let him come to Me and drink" (John 7:37). I thirst for more of You because I am in a dry place without You. I come to You this day and drink deeply of Your Spirit. I know You are everywhere, but I also know there are deeper manifestations of Your presence that I long to experience. I draw close to You today, grateful that You will draw close to me as You have promised in Your Word.

In Jesus' name I pray.

My Prayer for Me

Lord—I am so tired so thirsty too busy — Please help me to focus on You, drink deeply of what you offer 24 x 7 ☺

Help My Child Desire to
Live Your Way

*Blessed are those who hunger and
thirst for righteousness,
for they shall be filled.*

MATTHEW 5:6

Lord, I pray for (name of child) [TRENTON] to have an ever-increasing hunger for more of You. May ~~she~~ (he) grow to long for Your presence—long to spend time with You in prayer, praise, and worship. Give her (him) a desire for the truth of Your Word and a love for Your laws and Your ways. Teach her (him) to live by faith and be led by Your Holy Spirit, and to have a desire to live Your way. May a deep reverence and love for You and Your laws color everything she (he) does and every choice ~~she~~ (he) makes. Help her (him) to understand the consequences of ~~her~~ (his) actions. May she (he) learn to not be wise in ~~her~~ (his) own eyes, but rather to "fear the Lord and depart from evil" (Proverbs 3:7).

In Jesus' name I pray.

My Prayer for My Child

Lord - please crush Trentons "ego" "self" and prick his heart mind and soul for You. Bring the right people, friends, mentors into his life. Help me to be a guide and support to him.
Amen

13

Lord, Help Me to Know the Truth

I will pray the Father, and He will
give you another Helper,
that He may abide with you
forever—the Spirit of truth,
whom the world cannot receive, because
it neither sees Him nor knows Him;
but you know Him, for He dwells
with you and will be in you.

JOHN 14:16-17

Lord, I thank You that You have given me Your Spirit—the Spirit of truth—to be my Helper. I long to know You in every way You can be known, so help me to truly comprehend who You are and rely on You as my Helper who will lead me into all truth. I don't want to be a person who is "always learning and never able to come to the knowledge of the truth" (2 Timothy 3:7). I want to know the truth about who You are because I know You are near to all who call upon You in truth (Psalm 145:18). Teach me how to pray myself closer to You.

In Jesus' name I pray.

My Prayer for Me

_____

_____

_____

Plant Your Truth in My Child's Heart

A false witness will not go unpunished,
And he who speaks lies will not escape.

PROVERBS 19:5

Lord, I pray You will help (<u>name of child</u>) to know the difference between truth and lies. Deliver him (her) from any pride that makes him (her) believe that he (she) knows better than You. I pray he (she) will have a teachable and submissive spirit and be able to stand strong in truth. Write Your truth in his (her) mind and on his (her) heart so he (she) always walks with a confident assurance of the rightness of Your commands. As he (she) learns to pray, teach him (her) to listen for Your voice. May there always be a Holy Spirit fire in his (her) heart and an unwavering desire for You and Your truth.

In Jesus' name I pray.

My Prayer for My Child

_____

_____

_____

_____

_____

_____

Lord, Cleanse Me and Make My Heart Right Before You

*If we confess our sins, He is faithful
and just to forgive us our sins
and to cleanse us from all unrighteousness.*

1 JOHN 1:9

Lord, I come humbly before You and ask You to cleanse my heart and renew a right spirit within me. Forgive me for thoughts I have had, words I have spoken, and things that I have done that are not glorifying to You or are in direct contradiction to Your commands. Specifically, I confess to You (name any thoughts, words, or actions that you know are not pleasing to God). I confess it as sin and I repent of it. I choose to walk away from this pattern of thought or action and live Your way. I know You are "gracious and merciful, slow to anger and of great kindness" (Joel 2:13). Forgive me for ever taking that for granted.

In Jesus' name I pray.

My Prayer for Me

_____

_____

_____

_____

Make My Child Quick to Confess Wrongdoing

He who covers his sins will not prosper,
but whoever confesses and forsakes
them will have mercy.

PROVERBS 28:13

Lord, I pray You would give (name of child) a heart that is quick to confess her (his) sins. May she (he) easily recognize them and not even try to hide them. Help her (him) to be truly repentant of them so that she (he) can be forgiven and cleansed. Help her (him) to understand that Your laws, and my rules, are for her (his) benefit and that the confession and repentance You require must become a way of life. At the moment of recognition and repentance, may she (he) say as David did, "Create in me a clean heart, O God, and give me a right attitude" (Psalm 51:10, paraphrased). Take away all attraction to disobedience, and put in her (his) heart a desire to do the right thing.

In Jesus' name I pray.

My Prayer for My Child

_____

_____

_____

_____

Lord, Show Me the Truth About Myself

*I acknowledged my sin to You, and
my iniquity I have not hidden.
I said, "I will confess my transgressions to the Lord,"
and You forgave the iniquity of my sin.*

PSALM 32:5

Lord, "see if there is any wicked way in me, and lead me in the way everlasting" (Psalm 139:24). Show me the truth about myself so that I can see it clearly. I know I cannot hide anything from You, for You see everything. Nor do I want to hide anything. Help me to confess my sins to You quickly. I pray You will "have mercy upon me, O God, according to Your lovingkindness; according to the multitude of Your tender mercies, blot out my transgressions" (Psalm 51:1). Make me clean and right before You. I want to receive Your forgiveness so that times of refreshing may come from Your presence (Acts 3:19).

In Jesus' name I pray.

My Prayer for Me

Help My Child to Never Allow Secret Sin

*Beloved, if our heart does not condemn us, we have
confidence toward God.
And whatever we ask we receive from Him,
because we keep His commandments
and do those things that are pleasing in His sight.*
1 John 3:21-22

Lord, I pray You would bring to light any hidden sins in (name of child) so they can be confessed, repented of, and forgiven. Your Word says, "Blessed is he whose transgression is forgiven, whose sin is covered" (Psalm 32:1). I pray my son (daughter) will never be able to contain sin within him (her), but rather let there be a longing to confess everything. Keep him (her) from concealing any secret sins. May he (she) not live in guilt and condemnation, but rather dwell with a clear conscience understanding how great it is to be forgiven.

In Jesus' name I pray.

My Prayer for My Child

_____

_____

_____

_____

Lord, Help Me to Be a Forgiving Person

The discretion of a man makes him slow to anger,
and his glory is to overlook a transgression.

PROVERBS 19:11

Lord, help me to forgive others quickly. Show me when I am not doing that. If I have any anger, bitterness, resentment, or unforgiveness I am not recognizing, reveal it to me and I will confess it to You as sin. Specifically, I ask You to help me fully forgive (name anyone you feel you need to forgive). Make me to understand the depth of Your forgiveness toward me so that I won't hold back forgiveness from others. I realize that my forgiving someone doesn't make them right; it makes me free. I also realize You are the only one who knows the whole story and will see that justice is done, so I can release that person into Your hands.

In Jesus' name I pray.

My Prayer for Me

_____

_____

_____

_____

_____

_____

Teach My Child to Forgive Quickly

Forgive, and you will be forgiven.

LUKE 6:37

Lord, I pray You would help (name of child) to be a forgiving person. Help her (him) to understand the depth of Your forgiveness toward her (him) so that she (he) can be freely forgiving toward others. Teach her (him) to make the decision to forgive based on what You've asked us to do and not on what feels good at the moment. Give her (him) understanding that only You know the whole story about any of us, and that's why she (he) doesn't have the right to judge. Where she (he) has any unforgiveness, help her (him) to confess it to You so she (he) can move into all that You have for her (him).

In Jesus' name I pray.

My Prayer for My Child

_____

_____

_____

_____

_____

_____

_____

Lord, Give Me Wisdom to Make Right Decisions

*The mouth of the righteous speaks wisdom,
and his tongue talks of justice.
The law of his God is in his heart;
none of his steps shall slide.*

PSALM 37:30-31

Lord, I pray You would give me Your wisdom and understanding in all things. I know wisdom is better than gold and understanding better than silver (Proverbs 16:16), so make me rich in wisdom and wealthy in understanding. Thank You that You give "wisdom to the wise and knowledge to those who have understanding" (Daniel 2:21). Increase my wisdom and knowledge so I have discernment for each decision I must make. Please help me to always seek godly counsel and not look to the world and ungodly people for answers. Thank You, Lord, that You will always give me the counsel and instruction I need to stay on the right path.

In Jesus' name I pray.

My Prayer for Me

_____

_____

_____

_____

Give My Child Great Wisdom

A wise son makes a glad father,
but a foolish son is the grief of his mother.

PROVERBS 10:1

Lord, I pray You would give the gifts of wisdom, discernment, and revelation to (name of child). Help him (her) to trust You with all his (her) heart, not depending on his (her) own understanding, but acknowledging You in all his (her) ways so that he (she) may always hear Your clear direction as to which path to take (Proverbs 3:5-6). Help him (her) to be sensitive to the voice of the Holy Spirit saying, "This is the way, walk in it" (Isaiah 30:21). I know that much of his (her) happiness in life depends on gaining wisdom and discernment, which Your Word says brings long life, wealth, recognition, protection, enjoyment, contentment, and happiness. May all these things come to her (him) because of Your gift of wisdom.

In Jesus' name I pray.

My Prayer for My Child

_____

_____

_____

_____

_____

Lord, Teach Me to Walk in Obedience to Your Ways

*He who has My commandments and
keeps them, it is he who loves Me.
And he who loves Me will be loved by My Father,
and I will love him and manifest Myself to him.*

JOHN 14:21

Lord, Your Word says that those of us who love Your law will have great peace and nothing will cause us to stumble (Psalm 119:165). I love Your law because I know it is good and it is there for my benefit. Enable me to live in obedience to each part of it so that I will not stumble and fall. Help me to obey You so that I can dwell in the confidence and peace of knowing I am living Your way. My heart wants to obey You in all things, Lord. Please show me where I am not doing that. "With my whole heart I have sought You; oh, let me not wander from Your commandments!" (Psalm 119:10).

In Jesus' name I pray.

My Prayer for Me

_____

_____

_____

_____

_____

Give My Child a Heart That Desires to Obey

You are My friends if you do whatever I command you.

JOHN 15:14

$\mathcal{L}ord$, I pray You would give (name of child) a heart that desires to obey You. Put into her (him) a longing to spend time with You in Your Word, in prayer, and in listening for Your voice. I pray she (he) will value Your words that say we are Your friends, Jesus, when we do what You say. Don't allow her (him) to walk in pride, selfishness, and rebellion. By the authority You have given me in Jesus' name, I "stand against the wiles of the devil" and I resist idolatry, rebellion, stubbornness, and disrespect. They will have no part in my daughter's (son's) life, nor will my child walk a path of destruction because of them.

In Jesus' name I pray.

My Prayer for My Child

_____

_____

_____

_____

_____

_____

Lord, Help Me Understand Your Purpose for Me

*In Him also we have obtained an inheritance,
being predestined according to the purpose of Him
who works all things according
to the counsel of His will.*

EPHESIANS 1:11

Lord, thank You for the inheritance I have in You. Thank You that You have a great purpose for me according to Your will. I put my identity in You and my destiny in Your hands. I want what You are building in my life to last for eternity. I know that "all things work together for good" to those who love You and are called according to Your purpose (Romans 8:28). Show me clearly what You want to do in me and my life. Lead me in the way I should go so I will stay on the path You have for me. Help me do Your will and glorify You.

In Jesus' name I pray.

My Prayer for Me

_____

_____

_____

_____

_____

Give My Child a Sense of Purpose

*Eye has not seen, nor ear heard, nor
have entered into the heart of man
the things which God has prepared
for those who love Him.*

1 Corinthians 2:9

Lord, I pray (<u>name of child</u>) will find his (her) identity in
You. Give him (her) a vision for his (her) life when setting goals
for the future and a sense of purpose about what You've called him
(her) to do. Help him (her) to see himself (herself) as You do—so
that he (she) understands it is You "who has saved us and called us
with a holy calling, not according to our works, but according to
His own purpose and grace which was given to us in Christ Jesus
before time began" (2 Timothy 1:9). May his (her) commitment to
love You enable him (her) become all You created him (her) to be.

In Jesus' name I pray.

My Prayer for My Child

_____

_____

_____

_____

_____

_____

Lord, Strengthen Me to Stand Against the Enemy

Be strong in the Lord and in the power of His might.
Put on the whole armor of God,
that you may be able to stand
against the wiles of the devil.

EPHESIANS 6:10-11

Lord, I thank You for suffering and dying on the cross for me, and for rising again to defeat death and hell. My enemy is defeated because of what You have done. Thank You that You have given me all authority over the enemy, who is also Your enemy (Luke 10:19). Show me when I am not recognizing the encroachment of the enemy in my life. Teach me to use that authority You have given me to see him defeated in every area. Help me to fast and pray regularly in order to break any stronghold the enemy is trying to erect in my life or the life of my child. Thank You that by the power of Your Holy Spirit I can successfully resist the devil and he must flee from me (James 4:7).

In Jesus' name I pray.

My Prayer for Me

_____

_____

_____

Break Down Ungodly Strongholds Threatening My Child

*There is nothing covered that will not be
revealed, and hidden that will not be known.*

Matthew 10:26

Lord, I come to You on behalf of (<u>name of child</u>) and ask
that You would deliver her (him) from any ungodliness that may
be threatening to become a stronghold in her (his) life. I pray in the
name of Jesus that You will work deliverance in her (his) life wherever it is needed. I know that although "we walk in the flesh, we do
not war according to the flesh. For the weapons of our warfare are
not carnal but mighty in God for pulling down strongholds, cast-
ing down arguments and every high thing that exalts itself against
the knowledge of God" (2 Corinthians 10:3-5). I depend on You,
Lord, to show me anything I need to see regarding the enemy's possible threat to her (his) life.

In Jesus' name I pray.

My Prayer for My Child

_____

_____

_____

_____

_____

Prayer Couplet 10

Lord, Go Before Me as a Shield

He is a shield to those who walk uprightly;
He guards the paths of justice,
and preserves the way of His saints.

PROVERBS 2:7-8

Lord, I know in the midst of the battle I don't have to be afraid of the enemy since You are a shield for me because I live Your way. Thank You that even though the enemy tries to take me captive to do his will, You have given me the power to escape his snares completely (2 Timothy 2:26). Help me to "not be overcome by evil," but instead give me the strength to "overcome evil with good" (Romans 12:21). Hide me in the secret place of Your presence from the plots of evil men (Psalm 31:20). Thank You that the enemy will never bring me down as long as I stand strong in You.

In Jesus' name I pray.

My Prayer for Me

_____

_____

_____

_____

_____

_____

Be My Child's Protector

The Lord is my rock and my fortress and my deliverer;
My God, my strength, in whom I will trust, my
shield...I will call upon the Lord, who is worthy
to be praised; so shall I be saved from my enemies.

PSALM 18:2-3

Lord, I put (name of child) in Your hands this day. Be his (her) fortress, rock, strength, and shield when the enemy tries to encroach upon his (her) life. Be his (her) stronghold to whom he (she) runs in times of trouble. According to Your Word I thank You that You, Lord, will deliver him (her) from every evil work and preserve him (her) for Your heavenly kingdom (2 Timothy 4:18). Help me to pray in a way that protects him (her) from the plans of the evil one.

In Jesus' name I pray.

My Prayer for My Child

_____

_____

_____

_____

_____

_____

Lord, Show Me How to Take Control of My Mind

*Be renewed in the spirit of
your mind, and…put on the new
man which was created according to
God, in true righteousness and holiness.*

EPHESIANS 4:23-24

Lord, I don't ever want to walk according to my own thinking (Isaiah 65:2). I want to bring every thought captive and control my mind. I know Your Word is "a discerner of the thoughts and intents of the heart" (Hebrews 4:12). So as I read Your Word, show me any wrong thinking I have. May Your Word be so etched in my mind that I will be able to identify a lie of the enemy the minute I hear it. Spirit of truth, keep me undeceived. Help me to know the truth and identify all lies—in me and in others.

In Jesus' name I pray.

My Prayer for Me

_____

_____

_____

_____

_____

_____

Give My Child a Mind That Is Sound

God has not given us a spirit of fear,
but of power and of love and of a sound mind.

2 TIMOTHY 1:7

Lord, thank You for giving us a sound mind. I lay claim to that promise for (<u>name of child</u>). I pray her (his) mind will be clear, alert, bright, intelligent, stable, peaceful, and uncluttered. I pray there will be no confusion, no dullness, and no unbalanced, scattered, unorganized, or negative thinking. I pray her (his) mind will not be filled with complex or confusing thoughts. Rather, give her (him) clarity of mind so that she (he) is able to think straight at all times. Give her (him) the ability to make clear decisions, to understand all she (he) needs to know, and to be able to focus on what she (he) needs to do. Where there is now any mental instability, I speak healing in Jesus' name.

In Jesus' name I pray.

My Prayer for My Child

_____

_____

_____

_____

_____

_____

Lord, Transform My Thoughts so They Glorify You

Do not be conformed to this world,
but be transformed by the renewing of your mind,
that you may prove what is that good
and acceptable and perfect will of God.

ROMANS 12:2

Lord, I don't want to think futile and foolish thoughts or give place to thoughts that are not glorifying to You (Romans 1:21). Thank You that I "have the mind of Christ" (1 Corinthians 2:16). I want Your thoughts to be my thoughts. Show me where I have filled my mind with anything that is not of You. Help me to resist doing that and instead fill my mind with thoughts, words, music, and images that are glorifying to You. Help me to think upon what is true, noble, just, pure, lovely, of good report, virtuous, and praiseworthy (Philippians 4:8). I lay claim to the "sound mind" that You have given me (2 Timothy 1:7).

In Jesus' name I pray.

My Prayer for Me

_____

_____

_____

_____

Fill My Child's Mind with Godly Thoughts

To be carnally minded is death,
but to be spiritually minded is life and peace.

ROMANS 8:6

$\mathcal{L}ord$, I pray (<u>name of child</u>) will love You with all his (her) heart, soul, and mind so that there will be no room in him (her) for ungodly or worldly thoughts. I pray that his (her) faith in You and knowledge of Your Word will grow in him (her) daily. May Your Word take root in his (her) heart and fill his (her) mind with things that are true, noble, just, pure, lovely, of good report, virtuous, and praiseworthy (Philippians 4:8). Give him (her) great understanding so that what goes into his (her) mind from Your Word becomes part of him (her). Help him (her) to weigh carefully what he (she) sees and hears. May he (she) live his (her) life in the peace and soundness of mind You have for him (her).

In Jesus' name I pray.

My Prayer for My Child

_____

_____

_____

_____

_____

Lord, Take Me Deeper in Your Word

*He who looks into the perfect law of liberty
and continues in it, and is not a forgetful
hearer but a doer of the work, this one
will be blessed in what he does.*

JAMES 1:25

Lord, "Your Word is a lamp to my feet and a light to my path" (Psalm 119:105). Enable me to truly comprehend its deepest meaning. Give me greater understanding than I have ever had before, and reveal to me the hidden treasures buried there. I pray I will have a heart that is teachable and open to what You want me to know. Change me as I read it. Help me to be diligent to put Your Word inside my soul faithfully every day. Show me where I'm wasting time that could be better spent reading Your Word. Give me the ability to memorize it. Etch it in my mind and heart so that it becomes a part of me.

In Jesus' name I pray.

My Prayer for Me

_____

_____

_____

_____

_____

Teach My Child to Know More About You

All your children shall be taught by the Lord,
and great shall be the peace of your children.

ISAIAH 54:13

Lord, I pray (name of child) will have a deep reverence for You and Your ways. May she (he) hide Your Word in her (his) heart like a treasure, and seek after understanding like silver or gold. Instill in her (him) a desire to attain knowledge and skill, and may she (he) have joy in the process. Above all, I pray she (he) will be taught by You, for Your Word says that when our children are taught by You they are guaranteed peace. You have also said, "The fear of the Lord is the beginning of knowledge, but fools despise wisdom and instruction" (Proverbs 1:7). May she (he) never be foolish and turn away from learning, but rather turn to You for the true knowledge she (he) needs.

In Jesus' name I pray.

My Prayer for My Child

_____

_____

_____

_____

_____

Lord, Guide Me with Your Law

*Blessed is the man who walks not in the counsel of the
ungodly, nor stands in the path of sinners, nor sits in
the seat of the scornful; but his delight is in the law of
the Lord, and in His law he meditates day and night.
He shall be like a tree planted by the rivers of water
that brings forth its fruit in its season, whose leaf also
shall not wither; and whatever he does shall prosper.*

PSALM 1:1-3

Lord, may Your Word remind me of who You are and how
much You love me. May it bring the security of knowing who I am
in You and that my life is in Your hands. Thank You that when I
look into Your Word I find all I need for life. Give me ears to recognize Your voice speaking to me every time I read it (Mark 4:23).
When I hear Your voice to my heart and follow You, my life is full.
When I get off the path You have for me, my life is empty. Fill me
with Your Word every day so I stay on the path You have for me.

In Jesus' name I pray.

My Prayer for Me

_____

_____

_____

_____

Help My Child
Seek Guidance from You

*Take firm hold of instruction, do not
let go; keep her, for she is your life.*

PROVERBS 4:13

Lord, I pray (name of child) will have a heart that is open to Your Word and receives Your instruction. Teach him (her) to respect the wisdom of his (her) parents and be willing to be taught by them. Help him (her) to seek the counsel and instruction of godly people who are not scornful or dismissing of Your ways and laws. Teach him (her) to seek guidance in Your Word, and from those who know Your Word well, so that he (she) will be like a tree planted near water that brings forth fruit in its season and never withers or dies (Psalm 1:3). According to Your Word, I pray for my child: "May the Lord give you understanding in all things" (2 Timothy 2:7).

In Jesus' name I pray.

My Prayer for My Child

_____

_____

_____

_____

_____

Lord, Help Me Put My Life in Right Order

Seek first the kingdom of God and His righteousness,
and all these things shall be added to you.

MATTHEW 6:33

Lord, I pray You would help me set my life in right order. I want to always put You first above all else in my life. Teach me how to love You with all my heart, mind, and soul. Show me when I am not doing that. Show me if I ever lift up my soul to an idol. My desire is to serve You and only You. Remind me to always seek You and Your kingdom first, above all else, because I know when I do, everything will fall into place and my life will be in right order and You will supply the things I need.

In Jesus' name I pray.

My Prayer for Me

_____

_____

_____

_____

_____

_____

Teach My Child to Establish Godly Priorities

You will keep him in perfect peace,
whose mind is stayed on You,
because he trusts in You.

ISAIAH 26:3

Lord, I know You are a God of order and peace. And when things get out of order in our lives, even as children, we lose our peace. I pray for (names of children) that You would help them to make You a priority in their lives. Help them to understand that when they seek You first before anything else, then You will put their life in order, supply all their needs, and give them peace. Teach each one how to focus their mind and heart on You and shut out all else that attempts to distract them away from You. Give them strength and discernment to recognize the voice of their enemy and refuse to listen to it.

In Jesus' name I pray.

My Prayer for My Child

_____

_____

_____

_____

_____

Lord, Help Me to Cleanse My House

*Nor shall you bring an abomination into your house,
lest you be doomed to destruction like it.*

DEUTERONOMY 7:26

Lord, I pray I do not have anything in my house that is an abomination to You, but if I or someone else has brought something like that in, I pray You would reveal it to me now so that I can get rid of it. I do not want the destruction that will come upon it—or what it signifies—to come upon my home or my life. If anything that does not glorify You enters my home that I am not aware of, show me the truth and enable me to do the right thing to eliminate it. I don't want to accept something that is abhorrent in Your eyes all because I am ignorant of its significance. Teach me to know the truth.

In Jesus' name I pray.

My Prayer for Me

_____

_____

_____

_____

_____

_____

Fill My Child's Room with Your Presence

I will walk within my house with a perfect heart.
I will set nothing wicked before my eyes.

PSALM 101:2-3

Lord, I pray You would put Your complete protection over the room that belongs to (name of child). Fill her (his) room with Your love, peace, and joy. I pray that nothing will come into that room that is not allowed and approved of by You. If there is anything that should not be there, show me so that it can be taken out. I pray that You, Lord, will make this a holy place, sanctified for Your glory. You have said that "The curse of the Lord is on the house of the wicked, but He blesses the home of the just" (Proverbs 3:33). Bless the habitation of my child by filling our home and her (his) room with Your presence.

In Jesus' name I pray.

My Prayer for My Child

_____

_____

_____

_____

_____

_____

Lord, Prepare Me to Be a True Worshipper

*Whoever offers praise glorifies Me;
and to him who orders his conduct aright
I will show the salvation of God.*

PSALM 50:23

Lord, there is no source of greater joy for me than worshiping You. I come into Your presence with thanksgiving and bow before You this day. I exalt Your name, for You are great and worthy to be praised. "You have put gladness in my heart" (Psalm 4:7). All honor and majesty, strength and glory, holiness and righteousness are Yours, O Lord. You are "gracious and full of compassion, slow to anger and great in mercy" (Psalm 145:8). You are "mighty in power" and Your "understanding is infinite" (Psalm 147:5). Enable me to be a true worshipper and learn to always worship You in a way that always pleases and glorifies You.

In Jesus' name I pray.

My Prayer for Me

_____

_____

_____

_____

_____

Train My Child to Be a Grateful Worshipper

Because Your lovingkindness is better than life,
my lips shall praise You.

PSALM 63:3

Lord, help me to teach my children about Your love and kindness to us, and that it is better than anything else in our lives. I know that when they are grateful for all that You are and do, then they will want to worship You. Establish in each of them a thankful heart—appreciative of all You have done for us. Keep each one from the selfishness of heart that thinks they are entitled to all of the blessings they have been given, but rather let each heart be given over to grateful worship of You. Let worship and thanks to You be their first response to the things that happen in their lives.

In Jesus' name I pray.

My Prayer for My Child

_____

_____

_____

_____

_____

_____

Lord, Grow in Me Great Faith in You

According to your faith let it be to you.
MATTHEW 9:29

Lord, teach me how to walk by faith and not by sight (2 Corinthians 5:7). I need to be able to stand strong in Your Word no matter what is happening and not let any doubt have a place in me. Increase my faith greatly every time I read or hear Your Word. Help me to retain it. Make my faith strong as a shield that extinguishes the fiery darts of the enemy. I know that when I doubt I become like a sea wave that is tossed about by the wind. I don't want to be like that. Your Word says that "whatever is not from faith is sin" (Romans 14:23). Forgive me for the times I have doubt. Make me stronger in faith every day.

In Jesus' name I pray.

My Prayer for Me

_____

_____

_____

_____

_____

Plant in My Child Seeds of Strong Faith

If you have faith as a mustard seed, you will say to this mountain, "Move from here to there," and it will move; and nothing will be impossible for you.

MATTHEW 17:20

Lord, I pray (<u>name of child</u>) will be so strong in faith that her (his) relationship with You supersedes all else in life—even my influence as a parent. In other words, may she (he) have a relationship with You, Lord, that is truly her (his) own—not an extension of mine or anyone else's. I want the comfort of knowing that when I'm no longer on this earth, her (his) faith will be strong enough to keep her (him) "steadfast, immovable, always abounding in the work of the Lord" (1 Corinthians 15:58). I pray that she (he) will take the "shield of faith" in order to "quench all the fiery darts of the wicked one" (Ephesians 6:16). Help her (him) to grow stronger in faith every day.

In Jesus' name I pray.

My Prayer for My Child

_____

_____

_____

_____

Lord, Show Me the Gifts You Have Put in Me

Having then gifts differing according to the grace given to us, let us use them.

ROMANS 12:6

Lord, I pray You would show me what talents You have put in me and how I am supposed to use them. Help me to hear Your call upon my life. I know I am called to be a good mother because You have blessed me with a child (children). Help me to use the gifts You have given me in that way. But whatever it is You have called me to do, both now and in the future, I pray You will give me the strength and energy to get it done well. May I find great fulfillment and satisfaction in every aspect of it, even the most difficult and unpleasant parts. Help me to always use my gifts and talents to glorify You.

In Jesus' name I pray.

My Prayer for Me

Reveal My Child's Gifts and Talents

The gifts and the calling of God are irrevocable.

ROMANS 11:29

Lord, thank You for the gifts and talents You have placed in (name of child). Make them apparent to me and to him (her), and show me specifically if there is any special nurturing, training, learning experience, or opportunities I should provide for him (her). Your Word says, "Having then gifts differing according to the grace that is given to us, let us use them" (Romans 12:6). As he (she) recognizes the talents and abilities You've given him (her), I pray that no feelings of inadequacy, fear, or uncertainty will keep him (her) from using them according to Your will. May he (she) hear the call You have on his (her) life so that he (she) doesn't spend a lifetime trying to figure out what it is or miss it altogether.

In Jesus' name I pray.

My Prayer for My Child

_____

_____

_____

_____

_____

_____

Lord, Establish the Work of My Hands

Let the beauty of the Lord our God be upon us,
and establish the work of our hands for us;
yes, establish the work of our hands.

PSALM 90:17

Lord, thank You for the abilities You have given me. Where I am lacking in skill, help me to grow and improve so that I do my work well. Open doors of opportunity to use my skills and close doors that I am not to go through. Give me wisdom and direction about that. I commit my work to You, knowing You will establish it (Proverbs 16:3). I especially include the work I do as a mother. Help me to always do a good job in even the most difficult part of it. May it always be that I love the work I do and be able to do the work I love. Establish the work of my hands so that what I do will find favor with others, but most of all may it always be glorifying to You.

In Jesus' name I pray.

My Prayer for Me

_____

_____

_____

_____

_____

May My Child's Life Work Glorify You

Each one has his own gift from God,
one in this manner and another in that.

1 CORINTHIANS 7:7

Lord, I pray You would reveal to (name of child) what her (his) life work is to be and help her (him) excel in it. Bless the work of her (his) hands, and may she (he) be able to earn a good living doing the work she (he) loves and does best. Your Word says that each person has his or her own gift and that "a man's gift makes room for him, and brings him before great men" (Proverbs 18:16). May whatever she (he) does find favor with others and be well received and respected. But most of all, I pray the gifts and talents You placed in her (him) be released to find their fullest expression in glorifying You.

In Jesus' name I pray.

My Prayer for My Child

_____

_____

_____

_____

_____

_____

Lord, Enable Me to Bear the Fruit of Your Spirit

*The fruit of the Spirit is love, joy, peace,
longsuffering, kindness, goodness,
faithfulness, gentleness, self-control.
Against such there is no law.*

GALATIANS 5:22-23

Lord, I pray You would plant the fruit of Your Spirit in me and cause it to flourish. Help me to abide in You, Jesus, so that I will bear spiritual fruit throughout my life. Holy Spirit, fill me afresh with Your love today so that it will flow out of me and into the lives of others. You said in Your Word to "let the peace of Christ rule in your hearts" (Colossians 3:15). I pray Your peace would rule my heart and mind to such a degree that people would sense it when they are around me. Help me to "pursue the things which make for peace and the things by which one may edify another" (Romans 14:19). I pray the fruit of Your Spirit in me will always be evident to others, especially my children.

In Jesus' name I pray.

My Prayer for Me

_____

_____

_____

Fill My Child's Heart with Hope, Peace, and Joy

May the God of hope fill you with
all joy and peace in believing,
that you may abound in hope by
the power of the Holy Spirit.

ROMANS 15:13

Lord, I pray (<u>name of child</u>) be given the gifts of hope, peace, and joy. Let hope rise up in his (her) heart this day and may he (she) know the fullness of peace and joy that is found only in Your presence. Help him (her) to understand that true happiness and joy are found only in You. Whenever he (she) is overtaken by negative emotions, surround him (her) with Your love. Teach him (her) to say, "This is the day that the Lord has made; [I] will rejoice and be glad in it" (Psalm 118:24). Deliver him (her) from despair, depression, loneliness, discouragement, anger, or rejection. Keep these negative attitudes from having any place in his (her) life.

In Jesus' name I pray.

My Prayer for My Child

_____

_____

_____

_____

Lord, Help Me to Bear Good Fruit

*By this My Father is glorified,
that you bear much fruit;
so you will be My disciples.*

JOHN 15:8

Lord, I know that without You I can do nothing. Where I need to be pruned in order to bear more fruit, I submit myself to You. You are the vine and I am the branch. I must abide in You in order to bear fruit. Thank You for Your promise that if I abide in You and Your Word abides in me, I can ask what I desire and it will be done for me (John 15:7). Thank You for Your promise that says if I ask I will receive (John 16:24). I ask that You will make me like a tree planted by the rivers of Your living water so that I will bring forth fruit in season that won't wither (Psalm 1:3).

In Jesus' name I pray.

My Prayer for Me

_____

_____

_____

_____

_____

_____

Give My Child a Fruitful Life

For this reason we also, since the day we first heard
of it, do not cease to pray for you, and to ask that
you may be filled with the knowledge of His will
in all wisdom and spiritual understanding; that
you may walk worthy of the Lord, fully pleasing
Him, being fruitful in every good work.

COLOSSIANS 1:9-10

Lord, I pray You will cause my child to connect to You so that she (he) will live a fruitful life that glorifies You. Plant her (him) like a tree near Your living water so that she (he) will bear much fruit in each season of life that it is Your will for her (him) to do so. Help me to not cease praying for her (him) to have spiritual understanding and knowledge of Your will at all times. Enable her (him) to walk worthy of You and always live in a way that is pleasing to You. Bless her (him) in such a way that she (he) is consistently fruitful in everything she (he) does for Your glory.

In Jesus' name I pray.

My Prayer for My Child

_____

_____

_____

_____

Lord, Preserve Me in Holiness

He chose us in Him before the
foundation of the world,
that we should be holy and without
blame before Him in love.

Ephesians 1:4

Lord, You have said in Your Word that You did not call me to uncleanness, but in holiness (1 Thessalonians 4:7). You chose me to be holy and blameless before You. I know I have been washed clean and made holy by the blood of Jesus (1 Corinthians 6:11). You have clothed me in Your righteousness and enabled me to put on the new man "in true righteousness and holiness" (Ephesians 4:24). Help me to "cling to what is good" (Romans 12:9) and keep myself pure (1 Timothy 5:22). Lord, help me to separate myself from anything that is not holy. I don't want to waste my life on things that have no value.

In Jesus' name I pray.

My Prayer for Me

_____

_____

_____

_____

_____

Help My Child Be Attracted to What Is Holy

In a great house there are not only vessels of gold and silver, but also of wood and clay, some for honor and some for dishonor. Therefore if anyone cleanses himself from the latter, he will be a vessel of honor, sanctified and useful for the Master, prepared for every good work.

2 TIMOTHY 2:20-21

Lord, I pray You would fill (name of child) with a love for You that surpasses his (her) love for anything or anyone else. Help him (her) to respect and revere Your laws and understand that they are there for his (her) benefit. Hide Your Word in his (her) heart so that there is no attraction to what is not holy in Your eyes. I pray he (she) will run from evil, from impurity, and from unholy thoughts, words, and deeds. May he (she) be drawn toward whatever is pure and holy. Let Christ be formed in him (her) and cause him (her) to seek the power of Your Holy Spirit to enable him (her) to do what is right.

In Jesus' name I pray.

My Prayer for My Child

_____

_____

_____

Lord, I Want to Be Pure as You Are Pure

Blessed are the pure in heart, for they shall see God.
MATTHEW 5:8

Lord, help me to frequently examine my ways so that I can return to Your ways wherever I have strayed. Enable me to take any steps necessary in order to be pure before You. I want to be more like You. Make me a partaker of Your holiness (Hebrews 12:10), and may my spirit, soul, and body be kept blameless (1 Thessalonians 5:23). I know You have called me to purity, and You have said that "He who calls you is faithful, who will also do it" (1 Thessalonians 5:24). Thank You that You will enable me to stay pure so I will be fully prepared for all You have for me.

In Jesus' name I pray.

My Prayer for Me

_____

_____

_____

_____

_____

_____

_____

Lead My Child to Make Choices for Purity

Who may ascend into the hill of the Lord?
Or who may stand in His holy place? He who
has clean hands and a pure heart, who has not
lifted up his soul to an idol, nor sworn deceitfully.
He shall receive blessing from the Lord, and
righteousness from the God of his salvation.

PSALM 24:3-5

Lord, You have said, "Blessed are the pure in heart, for they shall see God" (Matthew 5:8). May a desire to have a pure heart be reflected in all my child does. I pray the clothes she (he) wears and the way she (he) chooses to adorn her (his) body and face will reflect a reverence and a desire to glorify You. Where she (he) has strayed from the path of purity, bring her (him) to repentance and work Your cleansing power in her (his) heart and life. Give her (him) understanding that living a life that is pure in Your eyes brings wholeness and blessing to her (him), and that the greatest reward for it is being closer to You.

In Jesus' name I pray.

My Prayer for My Child

_____

_____

_____

Lord, Move Me into the Purpose for Which I Was Created

*Be even more diligent to make
your call and election sure,
for if you do these things you will never stumble.*

2 PETER 1:10

Lord, I know Your plan for me existed before I knew You, and You will bring it to pass. Help me to "walk worthy of the calling with which [I was] called" (Ephesians 4:1). I know there is an appointed plan for me, and I have a destiny that will now be fulfilled. Help me to live my life with a sense of purpose and understanding of the calling You have given me. Take away any discouragement I may feel and replace it with joyful anticipation of what You are going to do through me. Use me as Your instrument to make a positive difference in the lives of those whom You put in my path.

In Jesus' name I pray.

My Prayer for Me

_____

_____

_____

_____

_____

Help My Child to Hear Your Calling

*Walk worthy of the calling with
which you were called.*

EPHESIANS 4:1

Lord, I pray You would pour out Your Spirit upon (<u>name of child</u>) this day and anoint him (her) for all that You've called him (her) to be and do. Deliver him (her) from any evil plan of the devil to rob him (her) of life, to steal away his (her) uniqueness and giftedness, to compromise the path You've called him (her) to walk, or to destroy the person You created him (her) to be. May he (she) not be a follower of anyone but You, but may he (she) be a leader of people into Your kingdom. Help him (her) to hear Your calling early in life so he (she) is not wasting time following anything that is not Your will. Help him (her) to clearly be aware of his (her) purpose.

In Jesus' name I pray.

My Prayer for My Child

_____

_____

_____

_____

_____

_____

Lord, Help Me to Walk in a Way That Pleases You

He who keeps His commandments
abides in Him, and He in him.
And by this we know that He abides in us,
by the Spirit whom He has given us.

1 JOHN 3:24

Lord, Your Word says that "if we say we have no sin, we deceive ourselves, and the truth is not in us" (1 John 1:8). I don't want to deceive myself by not asking You where I am missing the mark You have set for my life. Show me if I'm doing things I should not. Help me to hear Your specific instructions to me. Speak to me clearly through Your Word so I will know what's right and what's wrong. I don't want to grieve the Holy Spirit in anything I do (Ephesians 4:30). Help me to be ever learning about Your ways so I can live in the fullness of Your presence and move into all You have for me.

In Jesus' name I pray.

My Prayer for Me

_____

_____

_____

_____

Help My Children
Walk Submitted to You

My son, hear the instruction of your father,
and do not forsake the law of your mother;
for they will be a graceful ornament on your head,
and chains about your neck.

PROVERBS 1:8-9

Lord, Your Word instructs, "Children, obey your parents in all things, for this is well pleasing to the Lord" (Colossians 3:20). I pray You would turn the hearts of my children toward their parents and enable them to honor and obey both father and mother so that their lives will be long and good. Turn each heart toward You so that all they do will be pleasing in Your sight. May they learn to identify and confront pride and rebellion in themselves and be willing to confess and repent of it. Make them uncomfortable with sin. Help them to know the beauty and simplicity of walking with a sweet and humble spirit in obedience and submission to You.

In Jesus' name I pray.

My Prayer for My Child

_____

_____

_____

_____

Lord, Guide Me in All My Relationships

God sets the solitary in families;
He brings out those who are bound into prosperity.

PSALM 68:6

Lord, I lift up every one of my relationships to You and ask You to bless them. I ask that Your peace would reign in them and that each one would be glorifying to You. Help me to choose my friends wisely so I won't be led astray. Give me discernment and strength to separate myself from anyone who is not a good influence. I release all my relationships to You and pray that Your will be done in each one of them. I especially pray for my relationship with each of my family members, that You would bring healing, forgiveness, reconciliation, and restoration where it is needed. Make these relationships strong in You by the power of Your Spirit working in each of us.

In Jesus' name I pray.

My Prayer for Me

_____

_____

_____

_____

_____

Protect My Child's Relationships with Family Members

Blessed are the peacemakers,
for they shall be called sons of God.

MATTHEW 5:9

Lord, I pray for (<u>name of child</u>) and his (her) relationship with all family members. Protect and preserve them from any unresolved or permanent breach. Fill his (her) heart with Your love and give him (her) an abundance of compassion and forgiveness that will overflow to each member of the family. Specifically, I pray for a close, happy, loving, and fulfilling relationship between (<u>name of child</u>) and (name of family member) for all the days of their lives. May there always be good communication between them, and may unforgiveness have no root in their hearts. Help them to love, value, appreciate, and respect one another so that the God-ordained tie between them cannot be broken. Enable him (her) to be the peacemaker whenever possible.

In Jesus' name I pray.

My Prayer for My Child

_____

_____

_____

_____

Lord, Help Me Be Kind and Loving to Those Around Me

Be kind to one another, tenderhearted,
forgiving one another, just as God
in Christ forgave you.

EPHESIANS 4:32

Lord, I pray for any relationships I have with people who don't know You. Give me words to say that will turn their hearts toward You. Help me to be Your light to them. Specifically, I pray for (name an unbeliever or someone who has walked away from God). Soften this person's heart to open her (his) eyes to receive You and follow You faithfully. I also pray that I can show love, kindness, and forgiveness to those around me, especially to the women in my life who trust me to be consistently that way because they know I walk with You.

In Jesus' name I pray.

My Prayer for Me

_____

_____

_____

_____

_____

Help My Child to Be a Peacemaker

Behold, how good and how pleasant it is
for brethren to dwell together in unity!

PSALM 133:1

Lord, I pray You would teach my child to resolve misunderstandings quickly. I pray there would be no strain, breach, misunderstanding, arguing, or fighting, or bitter separating of ties in any relationship she (he) has. Give her (him) a heart of forgiveness and reconciliation. Your Word instructs us to "be of one mind, having compassion for one another; love as brothers, be tenderhearted, be courteous" to those around us (1 Peter 3:8). Help her (him) to do that. Help her (him) to live accordingly, "endeavoring to keep the unity of the Spirit in the bond of peace" (Ephesians 4:3). I pray You would instill a love and compassion in her (him) for all family members that is strong and unending, like a cord that cannot be broken.

In Jesus' name I pray.

My Prayer for My Child

_____

_____

_____

_____

_____

Prayer Couplet 29

Lord, Protect Me and All I Care About

*Because you have made the Lord, who is my refuge,
even the Most High, your dwelling place,
no evil shall befall you, nor shall any
plague come near your dwelling.*

PSALM 91:9-10

Lord, I pray for Your hand of protection to be upon me. I trust in Your Word, which assures me that You are my rock, my fortress, my deliverer, my shield, my stronghold, and my strength in whom I trust. I want to dwell in Your secret place and abide in Your shadow (Psalm 91:1). Keep me under the umbrella of Your protection. Help me never to stray from the center of Your will or off the path You have for me. Enable me to always hear Your voice guiding me. Send Your angels to keep charge over me and keep me in all my ways. May they bear me up, so that I will not even stumble (Psalm 91:12).

In Jesus' name I pray.

My Prayer for Me

_____

_____

_____

_____

_____

Place a Hedge of Protection Around My Child

When you pass through the waters, I will be with you; and through the rivers, they shall not overflow you. When you walk through the fire, you shall not be burned, nor shall the flame scorch you.

ISAIAH 43:2

Lord, I lift (name of child) up to You and ask that You would put a hedge of protection around him (her). Protect his (her) spirit, body, mind, and emotions from any kind of evil or harm. I pray specifically for protection from accidents, disease, injury, or any physical, mental, or emotional abuse. I pray he (she) will make his (her) refuge "in the shadow of Your wings" until "these calamities have passed by" (Psalm 57:1). Hide him (her) from any kind of evil influences that would come against him (her). Help him (her) to understand that You will be with him (her) wherever he (she) goes, and no matter what he (she) experiences, You will see him (her) through it.

In Jesus' name I pray.

My Prayer for My Child

_____

_____

_____

Lord, Be My Refuge and Strength

He who dwells in the secret place of the Most High
shall abide under the shadow of the Almighty.
I will say of the Lord, "He is my refuge and
my fortress; my God, in Him I will trust."

PSALM 91:1-2

Lord, You are my refuge and strength and "a very present help in trouble." Therefore I will not fear, "even though the earth be removed and though the mountains be carried to the midst of the sea" (Psalm 46:1-2). Protect me from the plans of evil people, and keep me from sudden danger. I thank You that Your mercy allows me to make my refuge in You because You love me and I trust You. Help me to dwell with You always in the secret place of Your shadow, so close to You that I can't be destroyed. Thank you for Your promises of protection that help me to sleep peacefully at night and experience a place of rest in the daytime as well.

In Jesus' name I pray.

My Prayer for Me

_____

_____

_____

_____

_____

Keep My Child Safe at All Times

I will both lie down in peace, and sleep;
for You alone, O Lord, make me dwell in safety.

PSALM 4:8

Lord, I thank You for Your many promises of protection. I pray You will put a hedge of safety and protection around (name of child) on every side and keep her (him) away from harm. Protect her (him) from any hidden dangers and let no weapon formed against her (him) be able to prosper. Help her (him) to walk in Your ways and in obedience to Your will so that she (he) never comes out from under the umbrella of that protection. Keep her (him) safe in all she (he) does and wherever she (he) goes.

In Jesus' name I pray.

My Prayer for My Child

_____

_____

_____

_____

_____

_____

Lord, Help Me to Forgive Others the Way You Forgive Me

*If you forgive men their trespasses,
your heavenly Father will also forgive you.*

MATTHEW 6:14

Lord, I don't want anything to come between You and me, and I don't want my prayers to be hindered because I have entertained sin in my heart. I choose this day to forgive everyone and everything and walk free from the death that unforgiveness brings. If any person has unforgiveness toward me, I pray You would soften their heart to forgive me and show me what I can do to help resolve this issue between us. I know that I cannot be a light to others as long as I am walking in the darkness of unforgiveness. I choose to walk in the light as You are in the light and be cleansed from all sin (1 John 1:7).

In Jesus' name I pray.

My Prayer for Me

_____

_____

_____

_____

Give My Child a Heart That Is Quick to Forgive

Whenever you stand praying,
if you have anything against anyone, forgive him,
that Your Father in heaven may also
forgive you your trespasses.

MARK 11:25

Lord, I pray (<u>name of child</u>) will never harbor resentment, bitterness, anger, or unforgiveness toward anyone. I also pray he (she) will forgive himself (herself) for times of failure, and may he (she) never blame You, Lord, for things that happen on this earth and in his (her) life. According to Your Word I pray he (she) will love his (her) enemies, bless those who curse him (her), do good to those who hate him (her), and pray for those who spitefully use and persecute him (her), so that he (she) may enjoy all Your blessings (Matthew 5:44-45). I pray he (she) will live in the fullness of Your forgiveness for him (her), and in the freedom of forgiveness toward others.

In Jesus' name I pray.

My Prayer for My Child

_____

_____

_____

Lord, Fill My Mind with Wisdom, Understanding, and Knowledge

*Through wisdom a house is built,
and by understanding it is established;
by knowledge the rooms are filled
with all precious and pleasant riches.*

Proverbs 24:3-4

Lord, You said in Your Word that You store up sound wisdom for the upright (Proverbs 2:7). Help me to walk uprightly, righteously, and obediently to Your commands. May I never be wise in my own eyes, but may I always fear You. Keep me far from evil so that I can claim the health and strength Your Word promises (Proverbs 3:7-8). Give me the wisdom, knowledge, understanding, direction, and discernment I need to keep me away from the plans of evil so that I will walk safely and not stumble (Proverbs 2:10-13). Lord, I know that in You "are hidden all the treasures of wisdom and knowledge" (Colossians 2:3). Help me to discover those treasures.

In Jesus' name I pray.

My Prayer for Me

_____

_____

_____

Help My Child to Always Make Wise Decisions

Happy is the man who finds wisdom,
and the man who gains understanding;
for her proceeds are better than the profits of silver,
and her gain than fine gold.

PROVERBS 3:13-14

Lord, Your Word says, "The fear of the Lord is the beginning of wisdom, and the knowledge of the Holy One is understanding" (Proverbs 9:10). May a healthy fear and knowledge of Your ways be the foundation upon which wisdom and discernment are established in (name of child). May she (he) turn to You for all decisions so that she (he) doesn't make poor choices. Help her (him) to see that all the treasures of wisdom and knowledge are hidden in You and that You give of them freely when we ask for them. As she (he) seeks wisdom and discernment from You, pour it liberally upon her (him) so that all her (his) paths will be peace and life.

In Jesus' name I pray.

My Prayer for My Child

_____

_____

_____

Lord, Strengthen Me to Resist Temptation

Blessed is the man who endures temptation;
for when he has been approved,
he will receive the crown of life
which the Lord has promised to those who love Him.

JAMES 1:12

Lord, do not allow me to be led into temptation, but deliver me from the evil one and his plans for my downfall. In the name of Jesus, I break any hold temptation has on me. Keep me strong and able to resist anything that would tempt me away from all You have for me. I pray I will have no secret thoughts where I entertain ungodly desires to do or say something I shouldn't. I pray I will have no secret life where I do things I would be ashamed to have others see. I don't want to have fellowship with unfruitful works of darkness. Help me, instead, to expose them to Your light (Ephesians 5:11).

In Jesus' name I pray.

My Prayer for Me

_____

_____

_____

_____

Keep My Child from Being Tempted

I have set before you life and
death, blessing and cursing;
therefore choose life, that both you
and your descendants may live.

DEUTERONOMY 30:19

Lord, I pray You would keep (name of child) free from any temptation—especially to alcohol, drugs, or any other addictive thing. Make him (her) strong in You and able to put You in control of his (her) life. Speak to his (her) heart, show him (her) the path he (she) should walk, and help him (her) see that protecting his (her) body from things that destroy it is a part of his (her) service to You. You have said that "if you live according to the flesh you will die; but if by the Spirit you put to death the deeds of the body, you will live" (Romans 8:13). Teach him (her) to live by the Spirit and not the flesh all the days of his (her) life.

In Jesus' name I pray.

My Prayer for My Child

Lord, Guard My Life from the Dangers of Temptation

No temptation has overtaken you except such as is common to man; but God is faithful, who will not allow you to be tempted beyond what you are able, but with the temptation will also make the way of escape, that you may be able to bear it.

1 CORINTHIANS 10:13

Lord, help me to hide Your Word in my heart so I will see clearly the temptations that threaten me. Help me to not sin against You in any way (Psalm 119:11). Thank You, Lord, that You are near to all who call upon You, and You will fulfill the desire of those who fear You. Thank You that You hear my prayers to be set free of all temptation. Deliver me from any weakness that could lead me away from all You have for me (Psalm 145:18-19). Thank You that You know "how to deliver the godly out of temptations" (2 Peter 2:9). Thank You that You will deliver me out of all temptation and keep it far from me because I trust in You.

In Jesus' name I pray.

My Prayer for Me

_____

_____

_____

Deliver My Child from Temptation to Do Wrong

There is a way that seems right to a man,
but its end is the way of death.

PROVERBS 16:25

Lord, I pray You would thwart any plan Satan has to destroy my child's life through alcohol and drugs. Take away anything in her (his) personality that would be drawn to those substances. I know children don't always see the seriousness of the dangers around them, but I pray You will open my child's eyes to the truth. Give her (him) discernment and strength to be able to say no to things that bring death and yes to the things of God that bring life. May she (he) clearly see the truth whenever tempted and be delivered from the evil one whenever trapped. May her (his) only addiction be to Your presence. Enable her (him) to stand strong and resist temptation so that she (he) will receive the crown of life You have promised.

In Jesus' name I pray.

My Prayer for My Child

_____

_____

_____

_____

Lord, Heal Me in Every Way

Heal me, O Lord, and I shall be healed;
save me, and I shall be saved,
for You are my praise.

JEREMIAH 17:14

Lord, thank You that You are the Healer. I look to You for my healing whenever I am injured or sick. I pray You would strengthen and heal me today. Specifically, I pray for (name any area where you need the Lord to heal you). Heal me "that it might be fulfilled which was spoken by Isaiah the prophet, saying: 'He Himself took our infirmities and bore our sicknesses'" (Matthew 8:17). Thank You that You suffered, died, and were buried for me so that I might have healing, forgiveness, and eternal life. By Your stripes, I am healed (1 Peter 2:24). In Your presence I can reach out and touch You and in turn be touched by You.

In Jesus' name I pray.

My Prayer for Me

_____

_____

_____

_____

_____

_____

Protect My Child from Injury or Disease

The prayer of faith will save the sick,
and the Lord will raise him up.

JAMES 5:15

Lord, because You have instructed us in Your Word that we are to pray for one another so that we may be healed, I pray for healing and wholeness for (<u>name of child</u>). I pray that sickness and infirmity will have no place or power in his (her) life. I pray for protection against any disease or injury coming into his (her) body. Your Word says, "He sent His word and healed them, and delivered them from their destructions" (Psalm 107:20). Wherever there is disease, illness, or infirmity in his (her) body, I pray that You, Lord, would touch him (her) with Your healing power and restore him (her) to total health.

In Jesus' name I pray.

My Prayer for My Child

_____

_____

_____

_____

_____

_____

Prayer Couplet 36

Lord, Help Me Learn Proper Body Care

*If anyone defiles the temple of God,
God will destroy him.
For the temple of God is holy,
which temple you are.*

1 CORINTHIANS 3:17

Lord, help me to be a good steward of the body You have given me. Teach me how to take care of myself. Lead me to people who can help or advise me. When I am sick and need to see a doctor, show me which doctor to see and give that doctor wisdom as to how to treat me. Enable me to discipline my body and bring it into subjection (1 Corinthians 9:27). I know that my body is the temple of Your Holy Spirit, who dwells in me. Help me to fully understand this truth so that I will keep my temple clean and healthy.

In Jesus' name I pray.

My Prayer for Me

_____

_____

_____

_____

_____

Help My Child Take Care of His Body

My people are destroyed for lack of knowledge.

HOSEA 4:6

Lord, I pray You would deliver (<u>name of child</u>) from any destruction, disease, or injury that could come upon her (him). Specifically I ask You to heal (name any specific problem). When and if we are to see a doctor, I pray You would show us whom that should be. Give that doctor wisdom and full knowledge of the best way to proceed. Thank You, Lord, that You suffered and died for us so that we may be healed. I lay claim to that heritage of healing You have promised in Your Word and provided for those who believe. I look to You for a life of health, healing, and wholeness for my child.

In Jesus' name I pray.

My Prayer for My Child

_____

_____

_____

_____

_____

_____

Lord, Free Me from Ungodly Fear

The Lord is my light and my salvation;
whom shall I fear?
The Lord is the strength of my life;
of whom shall I be afraid?

PSALM 27:1

Lord, I thank You that because You are my light and my salvation, and the strength of my life, I don't have to be afraid. I will be strong and of good courage, for I know You are with me wherever I go (Joshua 1:9). Free me from all ungodly fear, for I know fear is never of You. I pray You would guard my heart and mind from the spirit of fear. If I experience feelings of fear, I pray You would replace them with Your perfect love. If I have gotten my mind off of You and on my circumstances, help me to reverse that process so that my mind is focused on You.

In Jesus' name I pray.

My Prayer for Me

_____

_____

_____

_____

_____

_____

Deliver My Child from All Fear

I sought the Lord, and He heard me,
and delivered me from all my fears.

PSALM 34:4

Lord, I pray You will deliver (<u>name of child</u>) from any fear that threatens to overtake him (her). You said You have "not given us a spirit of fear, but of power and of love and of a sound mind" (2 Timothy 1:7). Flood him (her) with Your love and wash away all fear and doubt. Give him (her) a sense of Your loving presence that far outweighs any fear that would threaten to overtake him (her). Help him (her) to rely on Your power in response to his (her) prayers in a way that establishes strong confidence in Your love for him (her).

In Jesus' name I pray.

My Prayer for My Child

_____

_____

_____

_____

_____

_____

Lord, Help Me Serve You with Reverence

Teach me Your way, O Lord;
I will walk in Your truth;
unite my heart to fear Your name.

PSALM 86:11

Lord, Your Word says You will put fear in the hearts of Your people and You will not turn away from doing them good (Jeremiah 32:40). I know the only fear I need to have is the fear of what life would be like without You. That brings godly fear, which is deep reverence of You. "Oh, how great is Your goodness, which You have laid up for those who fear You" (Psalm 31:19). Thank You that Your unfailing love for me takes away all of my fears. Because I have received a kingdom that cannot be shaken, may I have grace by which to serve You acceptably with reverence and godly fear all the days of my life (Hebrews 12:28).

In Jesus' name I pray.

My Prayer for Me

_____

_____

_____

_____

_____

Teach My Child to Revere You

The fear of the Lord leads to life,
and he who has it will abide in satisfaction;
he will not be visited with evil.

PROVERBS 19:23

Lord, I know that as high as heaven is above the earth, that is how great Your mercy is toward those who revere You (Psalm 103:11). Help me teach my child to have great reverence for You all the days of his (her) life. Thank You that You will fulfill the desire of those who fear You, and You will hear our prayers (Psalm 145:19). I pray You would put in (name of child) a deep fear or reverence of You that is lasting. For I know that will help him (her) to make good choices, do the right thing, and stay away from evil (Proverbs 16:6). Please give him (her) strength to resist the influence of anyone who does not love and revere You and Your Word.

In Jesus' name I pray.

My Prayer for My Child

_____

_____

_____

_____

_____

_____

Lord, Use Me to Touch the Lives of Others

*By this we know love, because He
laid down His life for us.
And we also ought to lay down
our lives for the brethren.*

1 John 3:16

Lord, help me to serve You by helping others the way You want me to. Reveal to me any area of my life where I should be giving to someone right now. Give me a generous heart to give to the poor. Help me to be a good steward of the blessings You have given me by sharing what I have with people You instruct me to help. Show me whom You want me to extend my hand to at this time. Fill me with Your love for other people and help me to communicate it in a way that can be clearly perceived. Show me how to lay down my life in some way for another brother or sister in Christ as You instruct me. Your love for me helps me love others.

In Jesus' name I pray.

My Prayer for Me

_____

_____

_____

_____

Enable My Child to Touch Others for You

Those who are wise shall shine
like the brightness of the firmament,
and those who turn many to righteousness
like the stars forever and ever.

DANIEL 12:3

Lord, I lift up (<u>name of child</u>) to You and ask You to bring godly friends and role models into his (her) life. Give him (her) the wisdom he (she) needs to choose friends who never encourage him (her) to compromise his (her) walk with You in order to gain acceptance. Give me Holy Spirit–inspired discernment in how I guide or influence him (her) in the selection of friends. Your Word says, "He who walks with wise men will be wise, but the companion of fools will be destroyed" (Proverbs 13:20). Don't let my child be led astray by other people, but rather that he (she) will be one who leads others to You. Use him (her) to draw people into Your kingdom.

In Jesus' name I pray.

My Prayer for My Child

_____

_____

_____

Lord, Show Me How to Be a Blessing to Others

As each one has received a gift,
minister it to one another,
as good stewards of the manifold grace of God.

1 PETER 4:10

Lord, show me how I can be a blessing to others. I don't want to get so wrapped up in my own life that I don't see the opportunity to use the abilities You've given me to shine Your light and love to those around me. Show me what You want me to do and enable me to do it. Give me all I need to minister life, hope, help, and healing to people You put in my path. Make me to be one of Your faithful intercessors, and teach me how to pray in power for others. Help me to make a big difference in the world because You are working through me to touch lives for Your glory. May my greatest pleasure always be in serving You by serving others.

In Jesus' name I pray.

My Prayer for Me

_____

_____

_____

_____

_____

Teach My Child How to Help Other People

It is more blessed to give than to receive.

ACTS 20:35

Lord, I pray You would deliver (<u>name of child</u>) from anyone in her (his) life who has an ungodly character so that she (he) will not learn that person's ways and set a snare for her (his) own soul. Whenever there is grief over a lost friendship, comfort her (him) and send new friends with whom she (he) can connect, share, and be the person You created her (him) to be. Take away any loneliness or low self-esteem that would cause her (him) to seek out less than God-glorifying relationships. Teach her (him) how to be a good friend by being a giver instead of a taker. Enable her (him) to understand how to bless others by helping them at their point of need.

In Jesus' name I pray.

My Prayer for My Child

_____

_____

_____

_____

_____

_____

Prayer Couplet 41

Lord, Train Me to Speak Words That Bring Life

*Righteous lips are the delight of kings,
and they love him who speaks what is right.*

PROVERBS 16:13

Lord, help me be a person who speaks words that build up and not tear down. Help me to speak life into the situations and people around me, and not death. Fill my heart afresh each day with Your Holy Spirit so that Your love and goodness overflow from my heart and my mouth. Help me to speak only about things that are true, noble, just, pure, lovely, good, virtuous, and praiseworthy. Holy Spirit of truth, guide me in all truth. "Let the words of my mouth and the meditation of my heart be acceptable in Your sight, O Lord, my strength and my Redeemer" (Psalm 19:14). May every word I speak reflect Your love at all times.

In Jesus' name I pray.

My Prayer for Me

Fill My Child's Heart with Words That Please You

A good man out of the good treasure of his heart
brings forth good things, and an evil man
out of the evil treasure brings forth evil things.

MATTHEW 12:35

Lord, fill (name of child's) heart with Your Spirit and Your truth so that what overflows from his (her) mouth will be words of life and not death. Put a monitor over his (her) mouth so that every temptation to use profane, negative, cruel, hurtful, uncaring, unloving, or compassionless language would pierce his (her) spirit and make him (her) feel uncomfortable. I pray that obscene or foul language be so foreign to him (her) that if words like that ever do find their way through his (her) lips, they will be like gravel in his (her) mouth and he (she) will be repulsed by them. Help him (her) to always monitor himself (herself) so that words don't come out carelessly or thoughtlessly.

In Jesus' name I pray.

My Prayer for My Child

_____

_____

_____

_____

Lord, May I Always Speak Words That Honor You

Pleasant words are like a honeycomb,
sweetness to the soul and health to the bones.

PROVERBS 16:24

Lord, Your Word says that "the preparations of the heart belong to man, but the answer of the tongue is from the Lord" (Proverbs 16:1). I will prepare my heart by being in Your Word every day and obeying Your laws. I will prepare my heart by worshipping You and giving thanks in all things. Fill my heart with love, peace, and joy so that it will flow from my mouth. I pray You would give me the words to say every time I speak. Show me when to speak and when not to. And when I do speak, give me words to say that will bring life and encouragement.

In Jesus' name I pray.

My Prayer for Me

_____

_____

_____

_____

_____

_____

Teach My Child to Speak Words of Encouragement

Let the words of my mouth and
the meditation of my heart
be acceptable in Your sight, O Lord,
my strength and my Redeemer.

PSALM 19:14

Lord, I pray You would keep (name of child) from being snared by the words of her (his) mouth. You've promised that "whoever guards his mouth and tongue keeps his soul from troubles" (Proverbs 21:23). Your Word also says that "death and life are in the power of the tongue, and those who love it will eat its fruit" (Proverbs 18:21). May she (he) be quick to listen and slow to speak so that her (his) speech will always be seasoned with grace. Equip her (him) to know how, what, and when to speak to anyone in any situation. Enable her (him) to always speak words of hope, health, encouragement, and life, and to resolve that her (his) words will be pleasing to You.

In Jesus' name I pray.

My Prayer for My Child

_____

_____

_____

Lord, Lead Me into the Future You Have for Me

The path of the just is like the shining sun,
that shines ever brighter unto the perfect day.

PROVERBS 4:18

Lord, I put my future in Your hands and ask that You would give me total peace about it. I want to be in the center of Your plans for my life, knowing You have given me everything I need for what is ahead. I pray You would give me strength to endure without giving up. You have said that "he who endures to the end will be saved" (Matthew 10:22). Help me to run the race in a way that I shall finish strong and receive the prize You have for me (1 Corinthians 9:24). Help me to be consistent in prayer so that my life will be long, fruitful, and pleasing to You as well as others.

In Jesus' name I pray.

My Prayer for Me

_____

_____

_____

_____

_____

Give My Child a Great Future

This is the will of Him who sent Me,
that everyone who sees the Son and believes in Him
may have everlasting life; and I will
raise him up at the last day.

JOHN 6:40

Lord, I pray the future You have for (name of child) would be good, long, prosperous, and secure. I pray first for his (her) future in eternity. Put in him (her) a deep understanding of who You are. You have said in Your Word, "If you confess with your mouth the Lord Jesus and believe in your heart that God has raised Him from the dead, you will be saved" (Romans 10:9). I pray for that commitment of faith in You for my child. May he (she) call You his (her) Savior. Teach him (her) to acknowledge You in every area of his (her) life and always choose to follow You and Your ways so that his (her) life on earth will be blessed by You.

In Jesus' name I pray.

My Prayer for My Child

_____

_____

_____

_____

_____

Lord, Help Me to Put My Future in Your Hands

Those who are planted in the house of the Lord
shall flourish in the courts of our God.
They shall still bear fruit in old age;
they shall be fresh and flourishing,
to declare that the Lord is upright.

PSALM 92:13-15

Lord, I know Your thoughts toward me are to give me a future filled with hope and peace. I know You have saved me and called me with a holy calling, not according to my works, but according to Your own purpose and grace (2 Timothy 1:9). Thank You that You are always with me, guiding me on the path so that I won't lose my way. Help me to be so planted in You that I always flourish and bear fruit. I reach out for Your hand today so I can walk with You into the future You have for me.

In Jesus' name I pray.

My Prayer for Me

_____

_____

_____

_____

_____

Give My Child a Long and Good Future

*I know the thoughts that I think
toward you, says the Lord,
thoughts of peace and not of evil, to
give you a future and a hope.*

JEREMIAH 29:11

Lord, I thank You that Your thoughts toward my child are to give her (him) peace, hope, and a good future. Help her (him) to live in a way that is always deserving of that promise for her (his) life. I pray (<u>name of child</u>) will live a fruitful life, ever increasing in the knowledge of You. May she (he) always know Your will, have spiritual understanding, and walk in a manner that is pleasing in Your sight. Thank You that You care about her (his) future even more than I do and that it is secure in You. Give her (him) a future that is bright, long, prosperous, and secure. Guide her (him) step-by-step so that she (he) never gets off the path You have for her (him).

In Jesus' name I pray.

My Prayer for My Child

_____

_____

_____

Lord, I Ask for a Fresh Flow of Your Spirit in Me

*If you being evil, know how to give
good gifts to your children,
how much more will your heavenly
Father give the Holy Spirit
to those who ask Him!*

LUKE 11:13

Lord, pour Your Spirit on me in a fresh way. I need to hear Your voice speaking to my heart and guiding me every step of my life. I ask for Your power to work on my behalf, enabling me to do what I cannot do on my own. I need Your Spirit helping me to be stronger and better in every way. I know I cannot give to my children all that they need, but You can give them everything they need for life. I know that with a fresh flow of Your Spirit in me that I can be the best mom for them. Thank You that Your Spirit moving in my life will be a protective shield against all enemy opposition I face.

In Jesus' name I pray.

My Prayer for Me

_____

_____

_____

Pour Out Your Spirit on My Child

*It shall come to pass in the last days, says God,
that I will pour out of My Spirit on all flesh;
your sons and your daughters shall prophesy,
your young men shall see visions, your
old men shall dream dreams.*

ACTS 2:17

Lord, You have said that in the last days that You will pour out Your Spirit upon all flesh. I cry out to You from the depths of my heart and ask that You would pour out Your Holy Spirit upon my children. Pour out Your Spirit upon me and my other family members as well. Pour out Your Spirit upon whatever difficult circumstance each of my children face. Be Lord over every part of their lives and every aspect of their beings. Speak to their heart and help them to hear from You. Enable them to understand and recognize Your power working in their lives.

In Jesus' name I pray.

My Prayer for My Child

_____

_____

_____

_____

_____

Lord, Teach Me to Always Speak the Truth

Lying lips are an abomination to the Lord,
but those who deal truthfully are His delight.

PROVERBS 12:22

Lord, teach me everything I need to know about You. Enable me to exhibit faithfulness, gentleness, and self-control (Galatians 5:22-23). You are the Spirit of wisdom, grace, holiness, and life. You are the Spirit of counsel, might, and knowledge (Isaiah 11:2). Spirit of truth, help me to know the truth in all things. Thank You for leading and guiding me. Thank You for being my Helper and Comforter. Help me to pray powerfully and worship You in a way that is pleasing to You. Thank You that You will raise me up to be with You when my life on earth has ended. Until then, lead me ever closer to You.

In Jesus' name I pray.

My Prayer for Me

_____

_____

_____

_____

_____

Give My Child a Heart to Be Truthful

I have no greater joy than to hear
that my children walk in truth.

3 John 4

Lord, open my child's ears to hear Your truth so that he (she) will reject all lies. Whenever he (she) hesitates to do that, stretch out Your hand and draw him (her) back toward You. Convict his (her) heart about the lying spirit in the world today, and give him (her) the strength and clarity of conviction to reject it. Enable him (her) to rise above the onslaught of evil in our culture that has exchanged truth for lies. I pray Your Holy Spirit poured out on him (her) will completely neutralize the power of the enemy attempting to entice him (her) to lie. Teach him (her) to love Your truth more and more each day.

In Jesus' name I pray.

My Prayer for My Child

_____

_____

_____

_____

_____

_____

Lord, Open My Eyes to Understand Your Word

*I will worship toward Your holy
temple, and praise Your name,
for Your lovingkindness and Your truth;
for you have magnified Your word
above all Your name.*

PSALM 138:2

𝓛𝓸𝓻𝓭, I am grateful for Your Word. It shows me how to live, and I realize my life only works if I'm living Your way. Meet me there in the pages and teach me what I need to know. "Open my eyes, that I may see wondrous things from Your law" (Psalm 119:18). Thank You for the comfort, healing, deliverance, and peace Your Word brings me. It is food for my starving soul. Help me to read it every day so that I have a solid understanding of who You are, who You made me to be, and how I am to live. May Your words live in me so that when I pray, I will see answers to my prayers (John 15:7).

In Jesus' name I pray.

My Prayer for Me

_____

_____

_____

Help Me Teach My Child to Love Your Laws

Great peace have those who love Your law,
and nothing causes them to stumble.

PSALM 119:165

$\mathcal{Lord}$, I pray (name of child) will love Your Word and understand it more every day. Speak to her (his) heart whenever she (he) hears or reads it, and cause it to come alive to her (him). Teach her (him) Your ways and Your laws and enable her (him) to always choose to do the right thing. I pray a silencing of the enemy's voice to her (him) so that she (he) will hear Your Holy Spirit speaking to her (his) heart. You have said in Your Word that when someone turns his ear away from hearing the law, even his prayer is an abomination (Proverbs 28:9). I pray she (he) will never turn a deaf ear to Your laws.

In Jesus' name I pray.

My Prayer for My Child

_____

_____

_____

_____

_____

_____

Lord, Help Me to Always Remember That You Are My Hiding Place

You are my hiding place;
You shall preserve me from trouble;
You shall surround me with songs of deliverance.

PSALM 32:7

Lord, thank You that You are "my fortress, my high tower and my deliverer, my shield and the One in whom I take refuge" (Psalm 144:2). Thank You that "You have delivered my soul from death," and have "kept my feet from falling," so that I may walk before You (Psalm 56:13). Show me anything from which I need to be set free. I pray You "will deliver me from every evil work and preserve me" for Your kingdom (2 Timothy 4:18). "O God, do not be far from me; O my God, make haste to help me!" (Psalm 71:12). Help me keep in mind that I can always run to You and You will hide me from trouble.

In Jesus' name I pray.

My Prayer for Me

_____

_____

_____

_____

_____

Hide My Child from Enemy Attacks

Hide me under the shadow of Your wings,
from the wicked who oppress me,
from my deadly enemies who surround me.

PSALM 17:8-9

Lord, I am grateful that in You there is a place of safety. And I am well aware of the many dangers in this world today. I also know of the plans of the enemy for evil in my child's life. Only You can keep him (her) safe from trouble and hidden in Your presence. Only You can give him (her) a heart that understands how You love and protect Your children when they turn to You. I pray that whenever my child feels threatened, he (she) will run to You. Whenever he (she) senses the encroachment of evil into his (her) life, I pray he (she) will turn to You as his (her) shield. Help me to pray for him (her) as I ought to every day.

In Jesus' name I pray.

My Prayer for My Child

_____

_____

_____

_____

_____

_____

Lord, Hear Me When I Call to You in Times of Trouble

He shall call upon Me, and I will answer him;
I will be with him in trouble; I will
deliver him and honor him.
With long life I will satisfy him, and
show him My salvation.

PSALM 91:15-16

Lord, I pray that You will quickly respond to my prayers for help in times of trouble. I see that the forces rising up against Your believers are powerful, but I know You are far more powerful than they are. "You are my help and my deliverer; do not delay, O my God" (Psalm 40:17). When I cry out to You to liberate me from the enemy who tries to put me into bondage, I thank You that You will answer by setting me free (Psalm 118:5). Thank You that You will never lose interest in helping me but will continue to deliver me (2 Corinthians 1:9-10). Thank You that You will deliver me from all evil and be with me in every trial.

In Jesus' name I pray.

My Prayer for Me

_____

_____

_____

Teach My Children to Quickly Turn to You for Help

God is our refuge and strength,
a very present help in trouble.

PSALM 46:1

Lord, I pray my children will turn to You quickly in times of trouble. Help them to understand and believe that You are their refuge and source of strength, and You will hear them. I pray You will answer them quickly if they are in any danger. If the danger they are in involves the lies of the enemy encroaching upon them by advancing a wrong mind-set or an ungodly belief, open their eyes to see the truth. Shed Your light on whatever needs to be illuminated so they can clearly recognize the danger and run to You for help to resist and to step into the safety of Your presence.

In Jesus' name I pray.

My Prayer for My Child

_____

_____

_____

_____

_____

_____

Prayer Couplet 50

Lord, Enable Me to Stand Strong in You

He said to me, "My grace is sufficient for you,
for My strength is made perfect in weakness."
Therefore most gladly I will rather
boast in my infirmities,
that the power of Christ may rest upon me.

2 CORINTHIANS 12:9

Lord, I pray You would help me to stand strong in all I know of You. Teach me to believe Your Word no matter what is happening in my life. Enable me to be obedient to Your ways when I am tempted to not be. I acknowledge that I am weak, but I rejoice that You are strong in me—especially during times of difficulty. Enable me to learn what I need to know from each challenge I face. Lead me on the path You have for me. I don't want to take a single step without You. Help me in the difficult situation I am facing now. Lift me out of any hopelessness, fear, doubt, or frustration. Enable me to be firm in faith and always living in Your will.

In Jesus' name I pray.

My Prayer for Me

_____

_____

_____

Surround My Children with Your Angels

*The Lord shall preserve your going out and your
coming in from this time forth, and even forevermore.*

PSALM 121:8

𝓛𝓸𝓻𝓭, I pray You would surround my children with Your angels to keep watch over them so that they will not stumble (Psalm 91:12). Keep constant watch over them wherever they go. If they enter a path they should not go on, help them to hear Your voice leading them back to the path You have for them. Teach them to obey You so that they will always be in Your will and at the right place at the right time. I pray that "the fear of the Lord" will be for them a "fountain of life" that will serve to turn them "away from the snares of death" (Proverbs 14:27). I pray You will keep Your eyes on them and that they will not take their eyes off You. Help them learn to dwell in Your shadow where they are protected (Psalm 91:1).

In Jesus' name I pray.

My Prayer for My Child

_____

_____

_____

_____

Prayer Couplet 51

Lord, Teach Me to Rest in You Every Moment

My brethren, count it all joy when you fall into various trials, knowing that the testing of your faith produces patience. But let patience have its perfect work, that you may be perfect and complete, lacking nothing.

JAMES 1:2-4

Lord, thank You for helping me through every trial. Thank You that You have armed me with strength for the battle (Psalm 18:39). So many times "I would have lost heart, unless I had believed that I would see the goodness of the Lord in the land of the living" (Psalm 27:13). Help me to become so strong in You that I can rest in the midst of anything, no matter what happens, because I know You will give me what I need for the moment I am in. Teach me to "count it all joy" when I go through difficult times because of the perfecting work I know You will do for me (James 1:2-4). I know that "though I walk in the midst of trouble, You will revive me" (Psalm 138:7).

In Jesus' name I pray.

My Prayer for Me

_____

_____

_____

Help My Children Sense Your Presence and Protection

Though I walk through the valley of the shadow of death, I will fear no evil; for You are with me; Your rod and Your staff, they comfort me.

PSALM 23:4

Lord, I pray for Your hand of protection to be over my children. I pray they will put their trust in You as their shield and protector (Proverbs 30:5). Protect them physically from all accidents, diseases, infirmity, acts of violence by others, sudden dangers, and the plans of evil. Be their protector whenever they are in a car, plane, bus, boat, or any other means of transportation. Wherever they walk, I pray they will sense Your presence and protection. If they get on the wrong path, help them to see that immediately and turn to You to lead them away from danger (Psalm 17:5). I pray no weapon formed against them will prosper (Isaiah 54:17).

In Jesus' name I pray.

My Prayer for My Child

_____

_____

_____

_____

_____

Lord, Help Me Say No to Temptation

*Be sober, be vigilant; because your adversary the
devil walks about like a roaring lion, seeking
whom he may devour. Resist him, steadfast in
the faith, knowing that the same sufferings are
experienced by your brotherhood in the world.*

1 Peter 5:8-9

Lord, I pray You would lead me far away from all temptation to do or think anything that is not pleasing to You. Help me
to always know what is right and enable me to do it. Deliver me
from all attacks of the evil one, who tries to entice me away from
what is good in Your sight. I pray that the weakness of my flesh
will be overcome by the strength and power of Your Spirit in me. I
choose to be God-controlled and not flesh-controlled. I know that
I am dead to sin but alive in Christ Jesus, and therefore I will not
allow sin to reign in me. Help me to know Your Word well and
stand on it at all times.

In Jesus' name I pray.

My Prayer for Me

_____

_____

_____

_____

Protect My Child from Spiritual Pollution

*All that is in the world—the lust of the flesh,
the lust of the eyes, and the pride of life—
is not of the Father but is of the world.*

1 John 2:16

Lord, help my child to flee worldly pollution and resist the temptation to be drawn to it. Help her (him) to turn away from it, not look at it, and not be swayed by it. Give her (him) the conviction to change the channel; shut down the website; throw out the magazine, DVD, or CD; walk out of the theater; and not be with people who embrace sinful activity (Proverbs 27:12). Give her (him) understanding that any deviation from the path You have for her (him)—even if it's only occurring in the mind—will be a trap to fall into and a snare for her (his) soul. Enable her (him) to stand on the solid ground of what is right in Your sight. Help her (him) to hide Your Word in her (his) heart so that she (he) will not sin against You (Psalm 119:9-11).

In Jesus' name I pray.

My Prayer for My Child

_____

_____

_____

Lord, Help Me to Take Up the Shield of Faith

Stand therefore, having girded
your waist with truth...
above all, taking the shield of faith
with which you will be able
to quench all the fiery darts of the wicked one.

EPHESIANS 6:14,16

Lord, I declare that sin will not have dominion over me, for by Your power and grace I can resist it (Romans 6:11-14). I know I can't stand strong if I don't stand on the truth of Your Word. Give me great faith both in You and Your Word. Teach me to take up "the shield of faith," with which I will be able to "quench all the fiery darts of the wicked one" (Ephesians 6:16). Give me the ability to pray powerfully against all evil and strong faith to resist and withstand every onslaught of the enemy. Thank You for making a way for me to escape the enemy's plans for my destruction (1 Corinthians 10:13).

In Jesus' name I pray.

My Prayer for Me

_____

_____

_____

Teach My Child to Have Great Faith

All things are possible to him who believes.
MARK 9:23

Lord, You have said in Your Word that You have given each one of us "a measure of faith (Romans 12:3). I pray You would plant seeds of faith in my child and multiply them until he (she) has faith in You and Your Word that is strong enough to resist all inclination to have doubt. I pray his (her) faith will grow stronger every day and become a protective shield to him (her). I pray he (she) will be so strong in faith that his (her) relationship with You will supersede all else in his (her) life. Grow in him (her) a relationship with You that is truly his (her) own and not an extension of mine or anyone else's. Give him (her) faith that is steadfast and immovable, and help him (her) believe that in You all things are possible.

In Jesus' name I pray.

My Prayer for My Child

_____

_____

_____

_____

_____

_____

Lord, Help Me to Live in Your Will

*You have need of endurance,
so that after you have done the will of God,
you may receive the promise.*

HEBREWS 10:36

Lord, I commit my life to You. I want to always be in Your will in whatever I do. Help me to understand what is the hope of my calling (Ephesians 1:17-18). Enable me to "be steadfast, immovable, always abounding in the work of the Lord" that You have called me to do. I know my "labor is not in vain in the Lord"— as long as it's fulfilling Your perfect will for my life (1 Corinthians 15:58). Give me strength to resist any temptation to be led away from the center of Your will so I can move into everything You have promised to me in Your Word.

In Jesus' name I pray.

My Prayer for Me

_____

_____

_____

_____

_____

_____

Give My Child a Desire to Know Your Will

Not my will, but Yours, be done.
LUKE 22:42

$\mathcal{L}ord$, I pray (name of child) would have a sense of Your will for her (his) life and the ability to understand it clearly. Give her (him) the Spirit of wisdom so that the eyes of her (his) understanding will be enlightened. I pray Your plans for him (her) will succeed, and not the plans of the enemy. Enable her (him) to separate herself (himself) from all the distractions of this world and make choices to You in order to hear Your voice. I pray he (she) will say to You, "Lord, I want to do Your will and not my own."

In Jesus' name I pray.

My Prayer for My Child

_____

_____

_____

_____

_____

Lord, Show Me Your Purpose for My Life

*We know that all things work together
for good to those who love God,
to those who are the called according to His purpose.*

ROMANS 8:28

Lord, You knew me before I was born. Thank You that You predestined me to be saved and conformed to the image of Jesus. Thank You that You have called me and prepared me to glorify You (Romans 8:29-30). Give me a clear sense of Your purpose in my life. Help me to understand what is the hope of my calling and the exceeding greatness of Your power to enable me to fulfill that purpose. I pray that everything I do will support Your plans for my life. Show me the gifts You have put in me and how I can best develop them and use them for Your pleasure and high purpose. Help me to live every day with a deep sense of Your leading in my life.

In Jesus' name I pray.

My Prayer for Me

_____

_____

_____

_____

_____

Give My Child a Sense of Purpose

May He grant you according to your heart's desire,
and fulfill all your purpose.

PSALM 20:4

Lord, show me how to pray specifically for (name of child) so that he (she) will understand Your purpose and calling for his (her) life. When Your answer to what his (her) purpose is seems to be a long time in coming, help him (her) not to lose heart. Help me to encourage him (her) and give helpful input without being judgmental. Help him (her) to hear Your voice so he (she) will have a word in his (her) heart from You. Let it become a springboard propelling him (her) in the right direction. Give him (her) a strong sense of direction and purpose that transcends all fear, hesitation, laziness, temptation, defeat, and failure. Keep me strong in prayer until Your purpose has been fulfilled in his (her) life.

In Jesus' name I pray.

My Prayer for My Child

_____

_____

_____

_____

_____

_____

Lord, Help Me to Take Care of Myself

*Whether you eat or drink, or whatever you do,
do all to the glory of God.*

1 CORINTHIANS 10:31

Lord, I commit my body to You as a temple of Your Holy Spirit. Teach me how to care for it properly. Show me how I should eat and what I should avoid. Take away all desire for food that is harmful to me. Give me balance and wisdom. Help me to purify myself from everything that contaminates my body and spirit out of reverence for You (2 Corinthians 7:1). Enable me to obey You in this so I can live Your way and dwell in the peace You have for me. Show me where I allow unnecessary stress to rule in my life, and help me to take steps to alleviate it. Teach me to simplify my life, so that I can live better and be healthier.

In Jesus' name I pray.

My Prayer for Me

_____

_____

_____

_____

_____

_____

Enable My Child to Make Choices for Good Health

*If you diligently heed the voice of the Lord your God
and do what is right in His sight, give ear to His
commandments and keep all His statutes, I will put
none of the diseases on you which I have brought on
the Egyptians. For I am the Lord who heals you.*

EXODUS 15:26

Lord, I pray (<u>name of child</u>) will enjoy good health and a long life. Give her (him) the wisdom and knowledge necessary to recognize that her (his) body is the temple of Your Holy Spirit. Help her (him) to value good health as a gift from You and not take it for granted the way many young people do. Teach her (him) to be disciplined in the way of eating, exercising, and getting proper rest. I pray that good body care habits will be established early on in her (his) life. But where bad habits have already begun, I pray they would be broken in her (him). Reveal any truth she (he) needs to see and give her (him) understanding of that truth.

In Jesus' name I pray.

My Prayer for My Child

_____

_____

_____

Lord, Send Forth Your Word to Heal Me

They cried out to the Lord in their trouble,
and He saved them out of their distresses.
He sent His word and healed them,
and delivered them from their destructions.

Psalm 107:19-20

Lord, thank You for Your healing power on my behalf. Thank You for sending forth Your Word to heal me. Thank You for hearing my prayers. I believe You, Jesus, are the living Word. You paid the price on the cross to purchase healing for me. You took my infirmities and bore my sickness. There is healing in Your name, and I believe You are my Healer. I pray Your Word will come alive in my heart every time I read it, speak it, or hear it, and it will be medicine for my body. I praise You, Lord, for all Your promises to me of safety, protection, and healing. I choose to believe Your Word and have faith in You and Your power to heal.

In Jesus' name I pray.

My Prayer for Me

_____

_____

_____

_____

Watch over My Child's Health

He was wounded for our transgressions,
He was bruised for our iniquities; the chastisement
for our peace was upon Him, and by
His stripes we are healed.

ISAIAH 53:5

Lord, help my child to understand the price Jesus paid in order to save us and bring us healing. I pray he (she) will feel convicted if he (she) does not submit his (her) body to You and take care of himself (herself) (Romans 12:1). Help him (her) to value his (her) body enough to treat it well. Teach him (her) the right way to live. When he (she) is not feeling well, guide all doctors who see and treat him (her). Enable them to make the correct diagnosis and to know exactly what to do. Where healing seems to be a long time in coming, help us to not lose heart or hope, but to instead increase the fervency and frequency of our prayers to You for healing.

In Jesus' name I pray.

My Prayer for My Child

_____

_____

_____

_____

Lord, Help Me Find Your Grace in My Time of Need

*Let us therefore come boldly to the throne of grace,
that we may obtain mercy and find grace
to help in time of need.*

HEBREWS 4:16

Lord, I thank You that You are a God of mercy and grace. I give thanks to You because You are good and Your mercy is extended to me forever (Psalm 136:1). I ask You for mercy especially in the times that I am going through problems for which I blame myself. Your mercy extended to me is a sign of Your constant, deep, and unfailing love for me, and it tells me that You always have my back. Your undeserved kindness toward me, in that You saved me, has been Your greatest gift of grace to me. Help me to experience and recognize Your grace in my every struggle. Help me to remember that Your grace is always sufficient for me.

In Jesus' name I pray.

My Prayer for Me

_____

_____

_____

_____

_____

Crown My Child's Life with Your Tender Mercies

Bless the Lord, O my soul, and forget not all
His benefits: who forgives all your iniquities,
who heals all your diseases, who redeems
your life from destruction, who crowns you
with lovingkindness and tender mercies.

PSALM 103:2-4

Lord, I thank You that You forgive and heal and redeem our lives from destruction. I pray (name of child) will clearly see how You do that for her (him). Pour out Your loving-kindness and mercy upon her (him) and help her (him) to recognize them. I pray that when she (he) feels as if she (he) has done something wrong and doesn't deserve Your grace and mercy, that she (he) will still run to You to receive those gifts in times of trouble. Teach her (him) to understand that You always welcome her (him) to come before You with a humble and repentant heart because You love her (him) and will always be merciful toward her (him).

In Jesus' name I pray.

My Prayer for My Child

_____

_____

_____

Lord, Teach Me to Be a Good Friend to Others

Two are better than one,
because they have a good reward for their labor.
For if they fall, one will lift up his companion.

ECCLESIASTES 4:9-10

Lord, thank You for the people You have put in my life. Make all my good relationships stronger. Help me to handle the difficult ones in a way that pleases You. Remove any hopelessly destructive relationship from my life by either changing it for the better or by helping me to walk away from it. Give me wisdom about the friends I choose. Help me not to ever be in a relationship with anyone who will lead me off the path You have for me. If there is any relationship I have that is destructive for either of us, enable us both to change in order to make it better or help us to let it go. Teach me to be a good friend to others.

In Jesus' name I pray.

My Prayer for Me

_____

_____

_____

_____

_____

Help My Child to Choose His Friends Wisely

The righteous should choose his friends carefully,
for the way of the wicked leads them astray.

PROVERBS 12:26

Lord, I pray You would give (<u>name of child</u>) discernment when he (she) chooses his (her) friends. I pray he (she) will stay away from friends who are ungodly or who will be a negative influence on his (her) life. Strengthen him (her) to not be friends with anyone who is ungodly in order to gain acceptance. I pray that if there is any bad influence in his (her) life right now that You would either transform that person into Your likeness or move them out of the realm of influence in my child's life. Your Word says that whoever walks with wise people will be wise, and anyone who walks with fools will be destroyed (Proverbs 13:20). Cause my child to be drawn to the wise and godly.

In Jesus' name I pray.

My Prayer for My Child

_____

_____

_____

_____

_____

Lord, Keep Me from the Way of Evil

Discretion will preserve you;
understanding will keep you,
to deliver you from the way of evil.

PROVERBS 2:11-12

Lord, I pray You would give me wisdom and discernment so that I can identify evil the moment it presents itself. Keep me from being blinded to its destructive ways. Give me discretion so that I will always do that right thing and never compromise my walk with You. Give me clear understanding about Your ways so I will unfailingly identify the encroachment of sin and evil upon my life. I ask that You will always deliver me from the plans of the enemy before they are set in motion and attempt to establish any influence in me. Help me to always make the clear distinction between Your ways and the ways of the enemy.

In Jesus' name I pray.

My Prayer for Me

_____

_____

_____

_____

_____

Enable My Child to Resist Bad Influences

The highway of the upright is to depart from evil;
he who keeps his way preserves his soul.

PROVERBS 16:17

Lord, I pray that this worldly culture will not have a hold on my daughter (son). Sever any attachment in her (him) for the evil of this world and free her (him) to be attached only to You. Give her (him) the understanding that will deliver her (him) from the way of evil. Help her (him) to trust in You and Your power and not "give place to the devil" (Ephesians 4:27). I pray she (he) would seek Your guidance for her (his) life, and make You her (his) "hiding place" where she (he) will be preserved from trouble. I pray she (he) will always hear and obey Your voice to her (his) soul, saying, "This is the way, walk in it" (Isaiah 30:21).

In Jesus' name I pray.

My Prayer for My Child

_____

_____

_____

_____

_____

_____

Lord, Help Me Not Have Doubts About My Future

Surely there is a hereafter,
and your hope will not be cut off.

PROVERBS 23:18

Lord, there are so many frightening things happening in the world around me. Help me not to doubt that my future is secure in You, no matter what else is going on. Thank You for the great future You have for me because You love me (1 Corinthians 2:9). Thank You that I am never alone. Thank You that You never leave me or forsake me, and my future with You is always secure. Help me not become fearful when things become shaky. I know Your timing is perfect and Your ways are right. Help me trust that my hope in You will never be cut off.

In Jesus' name I pray.

My Prayer for Me

_____

_____

_____

_____

_____

_____

Give My Child a Future of Peace

Mark the blameless man, and observe the upright;
for the future of that man is peace.

PSALM 37:37

Lord, I pray for (name of child) to have a future that is good, long, prosperous, and secure because it is in Your hands. Thank You that Your plans for him (her) are to bring peace and hope and a productive future. Turn his (her) heart toward You so that he (she) always has Your will and Your ways in mind. Keep him (her) from wasting time on a pathway You will not bless. Help him (her) to run the race in the right way, so that he (she) will finish strong and receive the prize You have for him (her) (1 Corinthians 9:24). May nothing ever separate him (her) from You and the future of peace You have for him (her).

In Jesus' name I pray.

My Prayer for My Child

_____

_____

_____

_____

_____

_____

Prayer Couplet 62

Lord, Help Me to Never Give Up

Let us not grow weary while doing good,
for in due season we shall reap if we do not lose heart.

Galatians 6:9

Lord, keep me from becoming discouraged. Help me to cling to Your promises so that they are engraved on my heart and are alive within me. Enable me to "not remember the former things, nor consider the things of old" (Isaiah 43:18). I know You are doing a new thing in me. I pray it will "spring forth" speedily. I pray You will "make a road in the wilderness and rivers in the desert" for me (Isaiah 43:18-19). I know I'm often in a hurry for things to happen, and I ask You to forgive me when I have tried to put You on my schedule. I pray that by patience I will possess my soul (Luke 21:19). Help me to never give up, but rather to trust that You "will perfect that which concerns me" (Psalm 138:8).

In Jesus' name I pray.

My Prayer for Me

_____

_____

_____

_____

_____

_____

Keep My Child from Discouragement

*Consider Him who endured such hostility
from sinners against Himself, lest you become
weary and discouraged in your souls.*

HEBREWS 12:3

Lord, I pray my child will be able to "run with endurance the race that is set before us" always looking to Jesus (Hebrews 12:1-2). At the first sign of discouragement, help her (him) to remember all that You, Jesus, endured for her (him). Help her (him) to remember that You are "able to do exceedingly abundantly above all that we ask or think, according to the power that works in us" (Ephesians 3:20). Guide her (him) step-by-step so that she (he) never loses hope and wanders off the path You have for her (him). I pray that You—the God of hope—will fill her (him) with Your joy and peace so that she (he) will reject discouragement and "abound in hope by the power of the Holy Spirit" (Romans 15:13). Help her (him) to always find encouragement in You and Your Word.

In Jesus' name I pray.

My Prayer for My Child

_____

_____

_____

_____

Prayer Couplet 63

Lord, Help Me to Be Holy as You Are Holy

Grant us that we, being delivered from the hand of our enemies, might serve Him without fear, in holiness and righteousness before Him all the days of our life.

LUKE 1:74-75

Lord, help me to be holy as You are holy. Jesus, help me to walk as You walked on earth (1 John 2:6). Enable me to be an imitator of You (Ephesians 5:1). Wash me with Your holiness and cleanse me from the inside out by the power of Your Spirit in me. Reveal whatever is hidden within me that I need to be rid of—any attitudes, thoughts, or sin that must be gone from my life. Separate me from all that separates me from You, and help me get rid of anything in my life that does not glorify You. Give me the conviction and strength I need to step away from whatever is not compatible with Your holiness in me.

In Jesus' name I pray.

My Prayer for Me

_____

_____

_____

_____

Give My Child a Clean Heart

Create in me a clean heart, O God;
and renew a steadfast spirit within me.

PSALM 51:10

Lord, where my son (daughter) has walked away from You in any way, cause him (her) to return to You with his (her) whole heart (Jeremiah 24:7). Enable him (her) to become a new creation in Christ as You have said in Your Word (2 Corinthians 5:17). Give him (her) a heart of repentance—the kind of heart that is humble and turned toward You. Wherever there is any rebellion in her (him), I pray You would create in him (her) a clean heart and renew a right spirit within him (her). Take away all pride that allows him (her) to think that he (she) can live without You. Give him (her) a desire to want what You want and to become more like You.

In Jesus' name I pray.

My Prayer for My Child

_____

_____

_____

_____

_____

_____

Lord, Help Me to Be a Worshipper Who Pleases You

*Let us continually offer the sacrifice of praise to God,
that is, the fruit of our lips, giving
thanks to His name.*

HEBREWS 13:15

Lord, "who is like You, glorious in holiness"? (Exodus 15:11). You are mighty and have done great things for me. Holy is Your name (Luke 1:49). Help me to continually maintain a humble heart of worship before You. Purify my heart and mind so that I can be a partaker of Your holiness (Hebrews 12:10). You are worthy of all praise and honor and glory, for only You are holy. "O Lord, You are my God. I will exalt You, I will praise Your name, for You have done wonderful things" (Isaiah 25:1). I sing praise to You, Lord, and give thanks at the remembrance of Your holy name (Psalm 30:4). I worship You in the beauty of Your holiness (Psalm 29:2).

In Jesus' name I pray.

My Prayer for Me

_____

_____

_____

_____

Enable My Child to Have a Grateful Heart Toward You

Offer to God thanksgiving,
and pay your vows to the Most High.
Call on Me in the day of trouble; I will deliver you,
and you shall glorify Me.

PSALM 50:14-15

Lord, I pray for (name of child) and ask that You would give her (him) a heart of thanksgiving and praise toward You. I pray that just as it was said of Your good and faithful servant Daniel that "an excellent spirit was in him" (Daniel 6:3), may it also be said of my daughter (son) that an excellent spirit is in her (him). Teach her (him) to recognize all that You have done for her (him) and cause her (him) to want to thank You every day for all of that. Give her (him) a heart of worship and praise toward You so that You will be pleased. Thank You that You will deliver her (him) in times of trouble.

In Jesus' name I pray.

My Prayer for My Child

_____

_____

_____

_____

Lord, Help Me to Serve You by Taking Care of Myself

You were bought at a price;
therefore glorify God in your body
and in your spirit, which are God's.

1 CORINTHIANS 6:20

Lord, help me to rest at night as You created me to do, for I know that a "sound heart is life to the body" (Proverbs 14:30). Help me to exercise as I should so that my body stays strong. Where I have long-entrenched bad habits when it comes to proper care for my body, I ask You to reveal them all to me and enable me to take the necessary steps to get free. Help me to love and appreciate my body and not neglect it. Enable me to always choose life (Deuteronomy 30:19). I know that even though my flesh and heart may fail, You are the strength of my heart forever (Psalm 73:26). Enable me to go from "strength to strength" by the power of Your Spirit so that I will enjoy good health and better serve You (Psalm 84:7).

In Jesus' name I pray.

My Prayer for Me

_____

_____

_____

_____

Help My Child to Make Choices for Health

Present your bodies a living sacrifice,
holy, acceptable to God,
which is your reasonable service.

ROMANS 12:1

Lord, I pray my children will make wise choices when it comes to caring for their body. Enable them to see it as showing love and obedience to You, and as one of the ways they honor and glorify You. Teach them to see it as their reasonable service to You. Help them to know the truth about the way they are to live so that they can be free of unhealthful habits. I pray they will value the body You have given them and desire to take proper care of it. Teach them the right way to live. Show me how to help them and instill in them a desire for the things that keep them in good health.

In Jesus' name I pray.

My Prayer for My Child

_____

_____

_____

_____

_____

_____

Lord, Comfort Me in Times of Trouble

Blessed are the poor in spirit,
for theirs is the kingdom of heaven.
Blessed are those who mourn,
for they shall be comforted.

MATTHEW 5:3-4

Lord, help me remember that no matter how dark my situation may become, You are the light of my life and can never be put out. No matter what dark clouds settle on my life, You will lift me above the storm and into the comfort of Your presence. Only You can take whatever loss I experience and fill that empty place with good. Only You can take away my grief and pain and dry my tears. "Hear me when I call, O God of my righteousness! You have relieved me in my distress; have mercy on me, and hear my prayer" (Psalm 4:1). I want to stand strong in Your truth and not be swept away by my circumstances.

In Jesus' name I pray.

My Prayer for Me

_____

_____

_____

_____

_____

Comfort My Children
When They Suffer

Be merciful to me, O God, be merciful to
me! For my soul trusts in You; and in the
shadow of Your wings I will make my refuge,
until these calamities have passed by.

PSALM 57:1

Lord, You have said in Your Word that even though evil people try to destroy the righteous, You will not allow it (Psalm 37:32-33). Protect my children from any plans of evil. Be with them when they are in deep water. And when they are walking through the fire, enable them to not be burned or consumed (Isaiah 43:2). Guide them through every valley as You grow their trust in You. Teach them to hide themselves under the umbrella of protection You provide for all who love You and live Your way. Give them the discernment to recognize Your Spirit comforting them in troubling times. Help them not to lose heart, but to look to You as their source of help.

In Jesus' name I pray.

My Prayer for My Child

_____

_____

_____

Lord, Help Me Trust You to Answer When I Pray

Whatever things you ask in prayer,
believing, you will receive.

MATTHEW 21:22

Lord, help me to pray in strong faith. I want to always pray without doubting that You hear my prayers and will answer according to Your will. Help me to pray about not just my needs, but also the needs of others. Show me how to pray about everything. Enable me to "pray without ceasing" (1 Thessalonians 5:17). Help me to leave the things I pray about at Your feet and in Your hands. Teach me to trust You so much that I don't have preconceived ideas about the way my prayers must be answered. I know it's my responsibility to pray, and You will answer in the way You see is right. Help me to trust that You do hear my prayers and will answer in Your way and in Your time.

In Jesus' name I pray.

My Prayer for Me

_____

_____

_____

_____

_____

Help My Children Believe You Always Hear Their Prayers

The eyes of the Lord are on the righteous,
and His ears are open to their prayers;
but the face of the Lord is against those who do evil.

1 PETER 3:12

Lord, help my children fully understand the connection between living Your way and seeing powerful answers to their prayers. Enable them to see that they can't just go their own way, doing whatever they want outside of Your ways for their life, and expect that You will do their bidding. Teach them Your Word that says, "If I regard iniquity in my heart, the Lord will not hear" (Psalm 66:18). Open their eyes to fully comprehend that allowing any sin into their life causes You to not hear their prayers until they get right with You by humbling themselves before You and repenting of any wrongdoing. Cause them to understand that because You are all-knowing, they can keep no secrets from You.

In Jesus' name I pray.

My Prayer for My Child

_____

_____

_____

_____

Lord, Give Me Faith That Pleases You

*Without faith it is impossible to please Him,
for he who comes to God must believe that He is,
and that He is a rewarder of those
who diligently seek Him.*

HEBREWS 11:6

Lord, thank You for the gift of faith You have given me. Increase my faith every day as I read Your Word. Give me strong faith to believe for the answers to my prayers. I know that it is not about me trying to establish great faith on my own, but that faith comes from Your Spirit and Your Word. I know that "whatever is not from faith is sin," so I confess all doubt within me (Romans 14:23). Your Word says that anyone who doubts is unstable and double-minded and cannot please You (James 1:6-8). I pray You will make me to be strong enough in faith so that I please You.

In Jesus' name I pray.

My Prayer for Me

_____

_____

_____

_____

_____

_____

Give My Child Strong Faith in You and Your Word

Faith comes by hearing,
and hearing by the word of God.

ROMANS 10:17

Lord, teach (name of child) to walk by faith and not by sight. Help her (him) to hear Your Word and believe what it says so she (he) can stand strong in Your promises and not doubt. I pray her (his) strong faith will become a shield from the enemy that will "quench all the fiery darts of the wicked" (Ephesians 6:16). When she (he) prays, enable her (him) to "ask in faith, with no doubting" (James 1:6). Help her (him) to understand that doubt is a sin in Your eyes (Romans 14:23). Increase her (his) faith every day so that she (he) can do great things for Your glory.

In Jesus' name I pray.

My Prayer for My Child

_____

_____

_____

_____

_____

_____

Lord, Help Me to Comprehend Your Love for Me

God demonstrates His own love toward us,
in that while we were still sinners, Christ died for us.

ROMANS 5:8

Lord, thank You that You are the God of love. Thank You for loving me even before I knew You (Romans 5:8). Thank You that You loved me enough to send Your Son, Jesus, to die for me and take all that I deserve upon Himself. Thank You, Jesus, that You love me enough to give me life with You forever and a good life now. Help me to understand the depth and unconditional nature of Your love for me, for I know that a great dimension of my healing and wholeness can only happen in the presence of Your love. Enable me to open up and receive Your love in all the ways I have not recognized before. You are the love of my life and I cannot live a moment without You.

In Jesus' name I pray.

My Prayer for Me

_____

_____

_____

_____

_____

Cause My Children to Always Sense Your Love

We love Him because He first loved us.
1 John 4:19

Lord, enable me to show love for my children in a way that they can always perceive it. Help them to see Your love in me and be able to clearly comprehend that. I pray they will be drawn to Your love in their lives and recognize that Your love is pure, unconditional, unfailing, and always has their best interests at heart. In response to Your love for them, teach them to express their love to You with a heart of worship, praise, and thankfulness. I pray that loving You and thanking You will always come easily for them.

In Jesus' name I pray.

My Prayer for My Child

_____

_____

_____

_____

_____

Lord, Teach Me to Love Others the Way You Do

He who does not love does not know God,
for God is love.

1 John 4:8

Lord, I know that one of the ways I can show love for You is to live Your way. And one of the best ways to do that is to extend the love You have given me to others. I know I cannot love others the way You want me to without Your love in me changing my heart to become more like Yours. I ask that You would pour Your love into my heart in greater measure today so that it overflows toward others. I don't want any lack of love in me to make it appear that I don't know You. I want people to know that I know You by Your love in me for them.

In Jesus' name I pray.

My Prayer for Me

_____

_____

_____

_____

_____

_____

Help My Child Have a
Heart of Love for Others

*If God so loved us,
we also ought to love one another.*

1 John 4:11

Lord, I pray that my child will always have a heart of love for others. Help him (her) to understand Your love for him (her) in such a way that he (she) truly opens up to receive it every day. Show him (her) how Your love for him (her) and in him (her) requires that he (she) love others with that same love. Teach him (her) that part of fulfilling his (her) purpose in life is showing love for others the way You love us. If he (she) finds that hard to do, help me to demonstrate it clearly in my own life by the way I show love for him (her), and for others around me.

In Jesus' name I pray.

My Prayer for My Child

_____

_____

_____

_____

_____

Lord, Help Me to Hear the Promptings of Your Spirit

As many as are led by the Spirit of God,
these are the sons of God.

ROMANS 8:14

Lord, in Your presence everything makes sense. When I am with You, I feel Your peace, love, and joy rise in me. When I have not spent enough time with You, I greatly miss that priceless sense of the fullness of Your presence. I come before You and ask You to fill me afresh with Your Holy Spirit today. Cleanse me with Your living water. Wash away anything in my heart of doubt, fear, or worry. Take away everything in me that is not of You. Enable me to walk in the Spirit and not the flesh, and exhibit the fruit of Your Spirit (Galatians 5:16-17). Help me to always be led by Your precious Holy Spirit in me so that I never get off the path You have for me.

In Jesus' name I pray.

My Prayer for Me

_____

_____

_____

_____

_____

Guide My Children by Your Holy Spirit

*Those who live according to the flesh
set their minds on the things of the flesh,
but those who live according to the Spirit,
the things of the Spirit.*

ROMANS 8:5

Lord, Your Word says that Your Holy Spirit "bears witness with our spirit that we are children of God" (Romans 8:16). I pray for each of my children that in their spirit they will always sense that they are a child of Yours. I pray according to Your Word that You would pour out Your Spirit upon them and they will hear You speaking to them what they need to know, do, and say. Guide them in all they do. Don't let them become paralyzed with indecision because they don't have a word in their heart from You. Give them revelation that fills their minds and hearts with a vision for their lives that opens their eyes to what You are calling them to do.

In Jesus' name I pray.

My Prayer for My Child

Prayer Couplet 72

Lord, Help Me to Rely on Word

The word of God is living and powerful, and
sharper than any two-edged sword, piercing
even to the division of soul and spirit, and
of joints and marrow, and is a discerner of
the thoughts and intents of the heart.

HEBREWS 4:12

Lord, my delight is not in the counsel of the ungodly, but it is in Your law. Help me to meditate on Your Word every day and night so that I can be like a tree planted by a river that brings forth fruit and doesn't wither, so that whatever I do will prosper (Psalm 1:1-3). Enable me to live Your way so that my prayers are always pleasing in Your sight (Proverbs 28:9). I pray that Your Word will reveal what is in my heart and cleanse it of all evil, exposing anything that is not Your will for my life. Teach me the right way to live so that my life will work the way You intend for it to do.

In Jesus' name I pray.

My Prayer for Me

_____

_____

_____

_____

_____

Teach My Child to Live Your Way

If you abide in Me, and My words abide in you,
you will ask what you desire, and
it will be done for you.

JOHN 15:7

Lord, grow a heart of love in (<u>name of child</u>) for Your Word and Your ways. Breathe life into him (her) as he (she) reads Your Word so that it comes alive to him (her). Give him (her) strong faith in Your Word so that he (she) will trust it and draw life from it. I pray he (she) will never turn away from Your laws and make his (her) prayers an abomination to You, but rather he (she) will live by Your Word and let Your words live in him (her). And in doing that, he (she) will see Your answer to his (her) prayers.

In Jesus' name I pray.

My Prayer for My Child

_____

_____

_____

_____

_____

_____

Lord, Help Me Move into the Freedom You Have for Me

The Lord is the Spirit;
and where the Spirit of the Lord is,
there is liberty.

2 CORINTHIANS 3:17

Lord, I know that true liberty and freedom come from You and Your Spirit working in my life. Help me to live in the Spirit and not in the flesh. Teach me to dwell in Your presence through praise and worship and reading Your Word so that I can be set free from any and every desire I am held captive by that is not from You. Remind me to seek Your presence every morning before my day grabs my attention. I know I can always find freedom simply by coming before You in worship and praise. And when I have found freedom in my life, enable me to stand fast in the liberty by which You have made me free (Galatians 5:1).

In Jesus' name I pray.

My Prayer for Me

_____

_____

_____

_____

_____

Set My Child Free from Any Attraction to Sin

If the Son makes you free,
you shall be free indeed.

JOHN 8:36

Lord, I know that when we commit sins we become enslaved of sin (John 8:34). Keep (name of child) from ever being held captive by anything or anyone. I know that Your plans for her (his) life are for total freedom. Help her (him) understand that where You are, there is liberty. Teach her (him) to sense Your presence when she (he) worships and praises You, and every time she (he) seeks You in prayer. Help her (him) to know the truth of Your Word that sets her (him) free so she (he) will never become imprisoned by anything. Liberate her (him) from all attraction to sin of any kind. Keep her (him) from being blinded by lies of the enemy disguised as truth.

In Jesus' name I pray.

My Prayer for My Child

_____

_____

_____

_____

_____

Lord, Enable Me to Quickly Identify the Enemy's Work

You who love the Lord, hate evil!
He preserves the souls of His saints;
He delivers them out of the hand of the wicked.

PSALM 97:10

Lord, I thank You that You have given me victory over the enemy. Because I love You and hate the enemy's evil work, You have promised to deliver me from the hands of the wicked when I cry out to You. I ask that You would enable me to immediately identify the work of the enemy trying to encroach upon my life. Keep me from ever giving any opening to the enemy's work by allowing any sin in my life. Keep me undeceived. If I am entertaining anything in my mind, heart, or life that does not please You, set me free from that blindness.

In Jesus' name I pray.

My Prayer for Me

Protect My Children from Plans of the Enemy

"No weapon formed against you shall prosper,
and every tongue which rises against you
in judgment you shall condemn.
This is the heritage of the servants of the Lord,
and their righteousness is from Me," says the Lord.

ISAIAH 54:17

Lord, Your Word says that You came "to proclaim liberty to the captives" and "to set at liberty those who are oppressed" (Luke 4:18). I pray that wherever (name of child) has been held captive by the enemy's lies that You would set her (him) free. Where she (he) is being oppressed by the enemy's plans for her (his) destruction, I pray You would deliver her (him) from that torment. Break any stronghold that the enemy has erected against her (him). I pray that no weapon formed against my child will ever prosper. Keep her (him) free of all evil influences. Cause her (him) to quickly identify evil and run away from it to the safety of Your presence.

In Jesus' name I pray.

My Prayer for My Child

_____

_____

_____

Other Books by Stormie Omartian

The Power of a Praying® Parent

Stormie looks back at 20 years of parenting and seeing the power in praying for her children. In these easy-to-read chapters, she shares from personal experience as to how parents can pray for their children's safety, character development, relationship with God, and so much more.

The Power of Praying® for Your Adult Children

In this follow-up to *The Power of a Praying® Parent*, Stormie addresses areas of concern you may have for your grown children and shares how to effectively lift them up to God. It doesn't matter how young or old they are, you can rest in the power of God working through your prayers for them.

Prayer Warrior

For every Christian who wants a powerful prayer life that is more than just asking for blessings, bestselling author Stormie Omartian shows you how to pray with strength and purpose—prayers resulting in great victory, not only personally but also in advancing God's kingdom and glory.

Lead Me, Holy Spirit

God wants those who know Him to hear when He speaks to their heart through His Holy Spirit. He wants to help believers enter into the close relationship with Him they yearn for, the wholeness and freedom God has for them, and the place of safety they can only find by following His leading to the center of His perfect will.